ONE-POT COOKING FOR TWO

ONE-POT
COOKING FOR TWO

Effortless Meals for Your Sheet Pan,
Skillet, Slow Cooker, and More

Linda Kurniadi
Photography by Jim Franco

**ROCKRIDGE
PRESS**

Interior and Cover Designer: Tricia Jang
Art Producer: Sue Bischofberger
Editor: Ada Fung
Production Manager: Riley Hoffman
Production Editor: Melissa Edeburn/Kayla Park

Photography © 2019 Jim Franco. Food styling by Mollie Hayward.

ISBN: Print 978-1-64152-808-5 | eBook 978-1-64152-809-2

To my dear readers.
Thank you so much for your support.

Contents

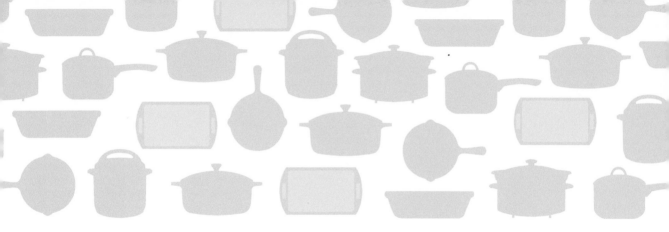

Introduction

EVERYONE HAS A FOOD STORY. I took food for granted until I moved to the United States from Indonesia and became a frugal student. Short on cash, but hungry, and haunted by memories of the tastes of my childhood, I began to try my own hand at cooking. Cooking at home was much cheaper than eating out, but more importantly, it reminded me of Indonesia, where my mom prepared meals for us every single day.

Looking back, I don't know how my mom was able to prepare all that food for the whole family while working a full-time job—she made not just one meal a day, but a minimum of two or three dishes for lunch and dinner. Meals were a time to gather around the table as a family. And as I write this cookbook, I think back to my parents and siblings eating and talking around the table, especially at dinnertime.

When I got married, I had to confront the fact that my husband and I have different cooking styles and skill sets, as well as different ideas about what constitutes a proper dinner. Whereas I was accustomed to variety, he wasn't, and we often ended up eating the same foods each day. That's when I decided I needed to get more creative in the kitchen. Thankfully, we agree on the importance of having dinner together as a family as often as possible. After the chaos of the day, cooking has become our way to unwind together. The heart of our home is the kitchen, the site of many delicious victories (as well as a few epic failures!).

My years of cooking for myself, and now for two, have shown me that cooking small batches can actually be trickier than cooking for a crowd. When I first started learning how to cook, I followed recipes made for four or six people, and I was often left with piles of leftovers. Bored with eating these same flavors again and again, I developed the skills and know-how to cook much smaller yields.

Many people, though, find cooking for oneself or for one's family difficult. A good number of people have told me how frustrated they are, for example, with the lack of time they have to get dinner on the table after coming home from a full day of work or school. We are all busy, so finding an hour (or longer!) to cook a nutritious and delicious meal can be hard, especially when you're only cooking for one or two.

This book proves that cooking dinner for two can be easy. All the recipes can be made in one pot, most take fewer than 45 minutes to make, and they use 10 or fewer main ingredients. You might think one-pot recipes can only be pasta dishes or casseroles, but with a little creativity you can make anything from sheet pan Crispy Kale and Shrimp Salad (see page 51) to electric pressure cooker Miso Salmon (see page 86).

In this book, you will find both casual weeknight recipes like fish tacos and a steak-and-potatoes sheet pan meal fit for a Friday date night. Cooking for two does not need to be complicated. Make this book your go-to cookbook for inventive and satisfying meals that are easy and quick to whip up.

One Pot, Two Plates, Three Meals a Day

When cooking a meal for two (or one) in a world filled with supersize recipes better suited for four or six people, the biggest concern is waste. You either quickly tire of eating the same thing three days in a row or end up throwing away food that has gone bad.

At the same time, we live in a fast-paced world where time is limited, and cooking a new dinner every night feels impossible. To all of you busy people out there—I feel you. I know that by the time you get home, you're tired and hungry and often don't feel like cooking. It's tempting to either order takeout or just warm up leftovers. But you have this book, and this means you are looking for solutions—you're in the right place. Luckily, you don't have to compromise.

In this chapter, I'll give you tips and tricks for how to plan, shop, and prep smartly so you can successfully cook for two, without the waste and stress.

PLANNING AHEAD FOR TWO

You'll want to start by choosing a day—most will find a weekend day best—to leisurely plan out your meals for the week (I promise, it won't take all day). Then:

MEAL PLAN AROUND MAIN INGREDIENTS. This may seem like common-sense advice, but sitting down and planning your meals for the week around the main proteins or ingredients you want to eat will allow you to eat a variety of dishes while limiting food waste and overspending at the grocery store. For example, if you are craving steak, you can turn one package of skirt steak into grilled steak for dinner one night and a steak salad for lunch another day.

SHOP WITH A LIST. Once you've chosen the meals you'd like to make, list the ingredients you'll need and include basic staples for your fridge, freezer, and pantry. Choose one day to go to the store each week to purchase those ingredients. Fresh ingredients like fish, meat, and leafy greens that won't keep for a week may require an additional trip.

STOCK UP ON GO-TO INGREDIENTS. I always make sure I have my go-to ingredients on hand. These ingredients help speed up my meal prep with-out skimping on flavor and quality. For example, store-bought pizza dough lets me bake my favorite pizzas at home anytime. I also make sure I have canned beans and lentils, good-quality jarred marinara sauce, and some versatile fresh and frozen fruits and vegetables on hand.

PREP AHEAD. Make a date with yourself (or each other!) to pull out your cutting boards and put your meal plans into action. This prep can be as simple as cutting up the veggies for a stir-fry, baking some sweet potatoes, or cooking a pot of chili so all you have to do is reheat on a busy Tuesday night. Tackling these tasks in advance saves you time during workdays.

BATCH-COOK AND FREEZE YOUR FAVORITE GRAINS. Batch-cooking and freezing your favorite grains saves time. Whole grains are simple to cook, and they freeze and reheat very well. Plus, they're versatile, so it won't feel like you're eating the same leftovers again and again. Cooked quinoa and brown rice, for example, can work both as quick side dishes and as bases of grain bowls or stir-fry meals.

SHOPPING SMART FOR TWO

Have you ever noticed your grocery store has been designed to entice you to purchase more than you need? Between the buy-one-get-one-free deals and family-size packs, economical food shopping for your small household can be tricky. Here are a few ways to downsize when food shopping:

BUY SMALL AND MAKE PEACE WITH THE PRICE TRADEOFF. For the most part, larger package sizes are the better deal. You will spend more per unit or ounce when you buy smaller quantities. But when you consider you might end up throwing out wasted food, the smaller packages often work out to be the same price. Look for half-packs of the items you'll need—rather than buying a dozen eggs, purchase just six. You could also buy a half-gallon of milk, or a half-loaf of bread. This will limit your waste and actually save money, even if it doesn't feel this way at first.

SHOP THE MEAT AND FISH COUNTER. Chicken, fish, and beef are typically packaged in one-pound-plus increments, which means you could be dealing with leftovers. Instead, ask the butcher or fishmonger for the exact amounts you'll need. Plus, shopping at the meat or fish counter can mean getting fresher and better-quality items than you'd get in pre-packed or frozen meat.

SHOP FOR PRODUCE CREATIVELY. Avoid pre-bagged vegetables rotting away in your crisper drawer by shopping for produce at a farmers' market if you have one nearby, or by perusing the loose bins at your grocery store. This way, if a recipe calls for one carrot, you won't need to buy a whole bag.

BUY THE "IMPERFECT" PRODUCE. Often, the vegetables or fruits that are "funny" sizes or shapes get ignored, or worse, thrown away because people are wary of buying imperfect produce. Where possible, look for undersized or even day-past-prime fruits and vegetables—they work well for your smaller portions and are often on sale, *and* you can feel good about helping combat food waste.

USE COUPONS WITH CARE. I am all about saving money and being thrifty, but coupons can trick you into purchasing something you don't need or buying more than you need. If you're determined to use coupons, though, focus only on pantry staples and things you already had on your list.

Six Tips for Using Up Ingredients and Minimizing Waste

STORE FOOD PROPERLY. Improper storage leads to a massive amount of food waste. Potatoes, tomatoes, garlic, cucumbers, and onions should never be refrigerated. These items should be kept at room temperature. A quick Google search will teach you how best to store your favorite perishables.

PICKLE YOUR PRODUCE. Have leftover vegetables? Pickle them for sandwiches and salads.

MAKE CREATIVE SWAPS. If a recipe calls for a small amount of an ingredient you don't have, check your fridge and pantry before running to the store. See if there's something you already have on hand to use as a substitute.

KEEP STOCKPILES CURRENT AND RELEVANT. Check your pantry regularly and be honest with yourself. If you don't plan on using something unopened, donate it to a food pantry or soup kitchen before its expiration date.

MAKE HOMEMADE BROTH OR STOCK WITH VEGGIE SCRAPS. Keep a bag in the freezer you can add to as you find yourself with scraps such as onion ends, wilted parsley, or withering peppers. Sauté them in a stockpot with butter or olive oil, add water for the broth, toss in some herbs and spices, and let them simmer away. Throw in your meat bones or a chicken carcass, too.

USE YOUR FREEZER WELL. The freezer can be used for so much more than storing leftovers. Store minced garlic, grated ginger, and grated cheese in small freezer bags. Chopped herbs can be frozen in olive oil in an ice cube tray. And bags of nuts can be frozen to prevent them from going rancid.

ONE-POT EASE

Once upon a time, one-pot cooking was the domain of campers, college students, and bachelors. The meals were simple, quick, and typically from a package. The idea was great—only one pot or pan to wash—but meals were usually unhealthy and uninspired.

One-pot cooking, though, can be the ideal option for two people. With just one pot, pan, slow cooker, electric pressure cooker (like the Instant Pot®), or skillet, you can prepare healthy, delicious, no-fuss, nutritious dinners that pack in flavor without the mess. And the best part? You can spend more time relaxing and unwinding after a long day instead of working in the kitchen.

ONE-POT COOKING EQUIPMENT

The one-pot cooking vessels I find most versatile and that I used to make the recipes in this book are:

8- OR 10-INCH NONSTICK SKILLET. Stainless-steel and cast-iron pans are perfect for caramelizing and searing if you don't mind the upkeep, but they can be finicky to care for. The most versatile and budget-friendly pan is a nonstick skillet, which you can use for everything from making eggs like my Kitchen Sink Omelet (see page 19), to quick stir-fry recipes like Crispy Tofu Summer Rolls (see page 61).

3-QUART POT OR SAUCEPAN. A quality pot or saucepan is vital to ensure your food is cooked through evenly. Find a saucepan that is a mixture of aluminum and stainless steel for its heating abilities and durability. Although it won't be the cheapest saucepan you can find, the money you spend will be worth it in the long term, especially if you enjoy soups like Quinoa Vegetable Soup (see page 39), and pasta dishes like Crabmeat Fettuccine (see page 82).

3.5- TO 5-QUART ENAMELED DUTCH OVEN.
A cast-iron Dutch oven that has been enamel-coated is a wonderful cooking vessel for braised dishes, soups, or stews like my Braised Chicken Cacciatore (see page 104). When used on a stovetop, the wide, tall sides allow for excellent heat retention and promise splatter-free, simple browning of veggies and meat. Best of all, this vessel transfers from stove to oven, making it perfect for dishes like Tuna Ravioli Lasagna (see page 88).

9-BY-9-INCH CASSEROLE OR BAKING DISH. A casserole or baking dish is a must-have for cooking batches of comfort food you can freeze and eat throughout the week. Meals like French Toast Casserole (see page 32) or Turkey Stuffed Pepper Casserole (see page 107) are great examples of this. Baking dishes are functional, durable, simple to clean, and economical—just what you want in cookware. A smaller square casserole dish is perfect for two, but if you cook larger portions for freezing, you may also wish to invest in a 9-by-13-inch casserole.

SHEET PAN. A standard rimmed half sheet pan (17.25-by-12.25-inch) and a med quarter sheet tray (13-by-9.5-inch) are two of the most versatile baking sheets for your home kitchen. They are inexpensive, durable, and lightweight. Having a few of each size in your cupboard is great for creating sheet pan meals like Sheet Pan Ratatouille Gnocchi (see page 71) and Sheet Pan Steakhouse Dinner (see page 122).

SLOW COOKER. The trusty slow cooker, also known as a Crock-Pot®, has been around since your grandma's time, and it is still a popular choice today for good reason. It is inexpensive and can turn cheap veggies or low-cost meat cuts into scrumptious, tender meals with the simple flip of a switch. What's better than being gone all day while your meal cooks itself at home? Although you can get much larger ones, a 3-quart slow cooker is just right for dishes like Slow Cooker Cinnamon Rolls (see page 30) and Braised Pork Tacos (see page 115).

ELECTRIC PRESSURE COOKER. Like a slow cooker, an electric pressure cooker has an inner pot that is heated with an electric element. Unlike a slow cooker, an electric pressure cooker speeds up the cooking process, allowing you to warm, steam, braise, simmer, and even slow cook faster—perfect for busy nights. Most modern electric pressure cookers, like the Instant Pot™, also allow you to sauté and brown meats and vegetables right in the inner pot. A 3-quart electric pressure cooker is the ideal size for two people. However, if you cook for more people every now and then, or want to batch-cook meals that freeze well, like Honey-Garlic Chicken Wings (see page 94) and Pressure Cooker Beef Stew (see page 124), a 6-quart model might be the way to go instead.

PREP TOOLS

Every recipe you make will start with prepping your ingredients. Here are the basic prep tools worth keeping handy.

SET OF KNIVES. If you can only have one thing for quick and efficient prep, I'd recommend a good set of knives. The chef's knife will quickly become your best friend because it can be used for almost any task in the kitchen. Paring knives are shorter than a chef's knife for more exact cutting and chopping. A serrated knife is perfect for cutting bread or tomatoes.

CUTTING BOARDS. If your budget allows, get a durable wooden cutting board. Wood is best for limiting bacteria and is kind to your knives. However, if you can't swing it, a plastic, heavy-duty board is perfectly fine. Look for one with rubberized grips.

MIXING BOWLS. A set of different-size mixing bowls is great for various prep work tasks. The cooking process feels so much more calm when your bowls of prepped ingredients are laid out neatly before you.

MEASURING SPOONS. Confession: Generally, I do not use measuring spoons. I'm accustomed to doing what my mom taught me—just eyeball it. However, I have learned using measuring spoons can mean the difference between success and failure, particularly in baking recipes.

PEELER. Vegetable peelers are great for taking the skins off cucumbers, zucchini, potatoes, and carrots. Most peelers can also cut veggies into ribbons, handy for making vegetable noodles (or "zoodles"), if you don't have a spiralizer.

RUBBER AND WOODEN SPATULAS. This trusty, multipurpose tool is good for scrambling eggs, tossing ingredients together on a sheet pan, making a stir-fry, and much more. Have a few rubber and wooden spatulas in your kitchen, and you'll be ready to make any recipe.

WOODEN SPOON. A good wooden spoon is essential for tasting soup, stirring sauce, and making creamy, seductive risotto. You'll want to have at least three or four.

STRAINER. When you need something that can strain all of the bits of aromatics out of stock or sauce, or drain rice or pasta, the humble strainer is the tool for the job. Choose one that's rust-resistant and fits snugly on top of your pots and bowls. These are relatively inexpensive; just make sure to find one with handles or hooks on the rims so it doesn't fall into the pot or bowl.

Fast Prep Hacks

When it comes to cooking, multitasking is hard, and trying to juggle too much is how things get burned. Luckily, I have a few prep hacks that will allow you to be more orderly and efficient.

PREP THE NIGHT BEFORE. Chop and prep all the ingredients for a slow cooker meal the night before, so in the morning you can just dump them in and go. Stock up on meal prep containers to keep prepped ingredients fresh.

LET SOMETHING ELSE DO THE CHOPPING. I use my food processor to quickly dice onions or carrots, instead of using a chef's knife. When cooking for two people, a medium-size food processor is sufficient. There are also manual food choppers, if you prefer.

MAKE AN ASSEMBLY LINE. Be organized. Have your recipe close by and easily accessible. Read it through before you start. Check that you have the right ingredients and tools and lay out your ingredients in the order you'll need them. Play some good music, and enjoy the process as you chop away.

CLEAN AS YOU GO. Keep your workspace picked up as you go and as things cook, so in the end you don't spend more time cleaning than cooking. Plus, a tidy workspace makes for a more organized and calmer cooking experience.

KITCHEN STAPLES FOR TWO

Who's inspired by an empty cupboard? Not me! Making sure you have a few kitchen staples on hand will ensure you remain excited about cooking and help you avoid grocery store trips for just a few items.

IN THE PANTRY

Nobody wants to break the bank on food. One key to saving on your grocery bill is making fewer trips to the store. Keep your pantry filled with basic, cheap ingredients so you can make meals at home—and change your dinner menu at the very last minute.

Here are some of the basics I try to keep on hand to easily create inexpensive meals.

CANNED BEANS. This staple comes in many varieties, packs a protein punch, and is an excellent way to bulk up soups, salads, stews, or a grain bowl.

PASTA. I am a pastaholic, and I like to keep a few varieties on my shelves for a quick and filling meal.

CANNED DICED TOMATOES. These are way cheaper than buying fresh tomatoes and are excellent in soups like Sausage and Lentil Soup (see page 43), stews, and curries.

JARRED MARINARA SAUCE. Jarred marinara sauce comes in handy for whipping up a pasta dish on the fly.

BOXED STOCK OR BROTH. Keep a couple boxes of stock or broth in your pantry so you can add flavor to soups or stews when you don't have time to make a homemade broth.

CANNED TUNA. Protein-packed tuna is an excellent source of the antioxidant selenium and a great addition to a salad for lunch or a pasta dish for dinner.

WHOLE GRAINS. Whole grains like quinoa, couscous, and brown rice make excellent side dishes or bases for a quick taco bowl or buddha bowl.

DRIED HERBS AND SPICES. Dried herbs and spices are great for adding flavor to a dish. Some of my favorites include curry powder, cumin, thyme, and rosemary—there are so many more, and all help make a dish unique.

IN THE FRIDGE AND FREEZER

Here are healthy staples I store in my fridge or freezer at all times.

BONELESS SKINLESS CHICKEN BREASTS AND THIGHS. Chicken breasts are leaner, but chicken thighs tend to be a bit cheaper and more flavorful. Most of the chicken recipes in this book call for chicken breasts, but you can easily substitute thighs—whichever you prefer.

WILD-CAUGHT SALMON FILLETS. We eat salmon twice a week. Since it's not realistic to get fresh salmon all the time, I keep individually wrapped salmon fillets in a resealable bag in the freezer; this way it's easy to defrost exactly what I need.

FRESH AND FROZEN VEGETABLES. Stock up on frozen vegetables like edamame, green peas, and vegetable medleys, and keep fresh staples like tomatoes, onions, bell peppers, and dark leafy greens on hand. This way, you will always have healthy options handy when you're cooking.

FRESH HERBS. Fresh herbs add flavor and freshness to almost any recipe. If the herbs are damp, wrap them in a dry paper towel before storing them. If they are dry, wrap them in a damp paper towel before storing.

EGGS. When you don't know what to eat at the end of a long day, breakfast for dinner is always a good idea. And eggs are so versatile and fast to cook—I recommend keeping at least six eggs on hand at all times.

GARLIC AND GINGER. Fresh garlic and ginger are excellent to have for flavoring savory dishes and can be handily stored in the freezer to keep from spoiling.

Perfect Pairings: Dishes that Can Be Prepared Simultaneously

Most of the recipes in this book are full meals on their own, but for those occasions when you want a little more food or are cooking for more than two people, here are some ideas for recipes that go well together and that can be made at the same time.

Recipe 1	Recipe 2	Prep Tip
Honey-Mustard Salmon Pastries with Asparagus (page 77)	Roasted Tomato Salad (page 45)	These can be baked at the same time and make for a great pairing. Just adjust your oven racks so both sheet pans fit (salmon on the top, tomatoes on the bottom).
Sheet Pan Ratatouille Gnocchi (page 71)	Honey-Garlic Chicken Wings (page 94)	Prep the wings the night before, and cook them at the same time the ratatouille goes into the oven.
Fried Egg and Pepper Sandwich (page 60)	Banana and Chocolate Pastries (page 31)	While the pastries are baking in the oven, cook up the sandwiches on the stove so you'll have a nice sweet treat waiting for you post-meal.
Balsamic-Glazed Steak Wraps (page 121)	Garlic Roasted Shrimp Salad (page 53)	Bring on that surf and turf in less than 30 minutes! Cook the steak on the stove while the shrimp are roasting in the oven.

ABOUT THE RECIPES

This book aims to build your confidence in the kitchen by making cooking for two simple, with easy-to-follow directions and recipes you'll want to make again and again. Some of these dishes might make a little more than two people will eat at one meal, but having some (not too many!) leftovers for the next day's lunch or to freeze for later isn't a bad idea.

All the recipes included in the book can be prepared in one pot, and each recipe includes an icon indicating the required cooking vessel. Recipes also may include one or more of the following labels.

SUPER QUICK. Takes no more than 30 minutes to prep and cook.

5-INGREDIENT. Uses five main ingredients or less (not including such staples as salt, pepper, flour, sugar, oil, butter, fresh garlic, or water).

COMFORT FOOD. For the times you're craving something a little more decadent.

GLUTEN-FREE, VEGAN, OR VEGETARIAN. Quickly find recipes that will work for your dietary needs. If you cannot eat gluten for health reasons, please be sure to check the labels of any packaged foods carefully to be sure all ingredients are safe for you to eat.

Most of the recipes also contain one of the following tips.

ADD IT. This tip suggests ingredients you might add to a recipe to make it heartier or more interesting.

COOKING TIP. This tip provides instructions for using an alternative cooking vessel than the one indicated at the recipe.

PREP HACK. This tip offers ways to prep a recipe in advance, save prep time on a dish, or reduce the number of tools or dishes used.

SWAP IT. This tip suggests potential substitutions to change a recipe's flavor, to replace a harder-to-find ingredient, or to make a recipe allergen-friendly, vegan, or vegetarian.

USE IT AGAIN. This tip promotes "zero waste" with suggestions for another recipe in which you can use the remainder of an extra ingredient.

Breakfast and Brunch

BREAKFAST RICE PUDDING

GLUTEN-FREE, SUPER QUICK, VEGETARIAN
PREP TIME: 5 MINUTES / COOK TIME: 15 MINUTES

This recipe came about on a chilly, rainy morning. I hadn't been to the grocery store in a week and really did not want to head out on this wet day. Instead, I scoured the cupboards trying to think up ideas. I eventually came across the ingredients for this creamy, slightly sweet, and oh-so-comforting breakfast.

1 cup long-grain rice, such as basmati

1 cup whole milk

1 cup cold water

¼ cup sweetened condensed milk

1 teaspoon cinnamon

1 teaspoon vanilla extract

Pinch salt

Raisins, for topping

1. Rinse the rice under cold running water and drain in a strainer.

2. Add the whole milk, water, and rice to an electric pressure cooker. Stir to combine.

3. Cover and cook on high pressure for 3 minutes. Once done, let the pressure release naturally, about 10 minutes. Turn off the pressure cooker and open the lid.

4. Add the condensed milk, cinnamon, vanilla, and salt. Stir well until combined and creamy.

5. To serve, divide the rice pudding into bowls and top with raisins.

SWAP IT: For a richer and more decadent rice pudding, swap out the cup of water for another cup of milk.

Per Serving: Calories: 597; Total fat: 8g; Total carbs: 116g; Protein: 14g; Fiber: 3g; Sugar: 38g; Sodium: 182mg

STRAWBERRY AND COCONUT OATS

COMFORT FOOD, VEGAN

PREP TIME: 5 MINUTES / COOK TIME: 7 HOURS

These strawberry and coconut oats are super simple to make with the help of your slow cooker—just pop the ingredients in the night before, go to sleep, and wake up to the smell of a delicious breakfast already made for you! Finish them off with maple syrup, shredded coconut, and a combination of your favorite berries for a sweet, nutty, and creamy breakfast.

1 teaspoon coconut oil

½ cup rolled oats

2 cups coconut milk

½ teaspoon cinnamon

½ teaspoon vanilla extract

Pinch salt

½ tablespoon maple syrup (optional)

½ cup strawberries, sliced, or other berries

1 tablespoon shredded unsweetened coconut

1. Turn on the slow cooker. Add the coconut oil and let it melt.

2. Add the oats, coconut milk, cinnamon, vanilla, and salt. Stir to combine.

3. Cook on low for 7 hours. Stir in the maple syrup (if using) and top with the strawberries and shredded coconut. Serve warm.

SWAP IT: Craving tropical flavors? Simply swap the strawberries for chopped pineapple, mango, or banana.

Per Serving: Calories: 678; Total fat: 62g; Total carbs: 31g; Protein: 9g; Fiber: 9g; Sugar: 11g; Sodium: 116mg

BACON AND VEGGIE SCRAMBLE

SUPER QUICK, GLUTEN-FREE
PREP TIME: 10 MINUTES / COOK TIME: 20 MINUTES

I'm a weeknight cook—almost exclusively. My weekends are reserved for spending time with family or trying out a new place to eat. I don't make breakfast often, but when I do, I like my meals to be quick and easy to prepare, without tasting like they are. This bacon and veggie scramble is colorful and bursts with flavor, and could not be easier to make.

4 large eggs

1 teaspoon chopped
   fresh basil

Salt

Freshly ground
   black pepper

4 bacon slices,
   coarsely chopped

¼ red bell pepper, seeded
   and diced

¼ small onion, diced

1 cup baby spinach

1. In a medium bowl, whisk the eggs and basil. Season with salt and pepper and set aside.

2. Place the chopped bacon in a skillet over medium-high heat, and cook until the bacon begins to look cooked but isn't crisp, about 5 minutes. Drain off the excess bacon fat.

3. Add the bell pepper and onion to the skillet, and cook until they start to soften, about 5 minutes.

4. Add the spinach and stir for 1 to 2 minutes, then pour the eggs over the vegetables and bacon. Reduce heat to medium-low. Tilt the skillet so the egg spreads across the bottom.

5. Cook, stirring frequently, for 5 to 8 minutes, or until the eggs are cooked through. Serve hot.

Per Serving: Calories: 388; Total fat: 32g; Total carbs: 4g; Protein: 20g; Fiber: 1g; Sugar: 2g; Sodium: 601mg

KITCHEN SINK OMELET

SUPER QUICK, GLUTEN-FREE
PREP TIME: 15 MINUTES / COOK TIME: 15 MINUTES

This omelet is so incredibly simple to make. Though I've provided measurements, I don't even really measure anything when I make this recipe—I just taste a little bit, add some more seasonings, and adjust accordingly. This technique is a good way to clean out the fridge while making something delicious.

3 large eggs

Salt

Freshly ground
  black pepper

2 tablespoons extra-virgin
  olive oil, divided

2 garlic cloves,
  finely minced

2 hot Italian sausages,
  casings removed

1 cup sliced white
  mushrooms

½ cup diced zucchini

3 cups baby spinach

1 plum tomato, finely diced

½ cup cheddar cheese,
  finely grated

1. In a medium bowl, whisk the eggs. Season with salt and pepper.

2. Heat 1 tablespoon of the oil in a skillet over medium-high heat. Add garlic and cook, stirring frequently, for 2 minutes. Add the sausage, breaking the pieces apart, and cook for 3 to 5 minutes. Transfer the garlic and sausage to a bowl.

3. Add the mushrooms and zucchini to the skillet, and cook, stirring frequently for 2 minutes. Add the spinach and cook until wilted, about 1 minute.

4. Transfer the vegetables to the same bowl as the sausage mixture. Add the tomato, and season with additional salt.

KITCHEN SINK OMELET Continues

5. Reduce the heat to medium-low. Pour the remaining 1 tablespoon oil into the skillet, then add the eggs. Cook, without stirring, until the edges are set, 1 to 2 minutes. Use a spatula to lift the edge of the omelet, pushing it toward the center and tilting the pan to allow the uncooked eggs to run underneath. Cook until the omelet is just set, 2 to 3 minutes.

6. Add the sausage and veggie mixture to one half of the omelet, sprinkle the cheddar cheese on top, and fold the other half of the omelet over the top. With a spatula, gently press down on the top to seal the omelet, and cook for another 1 to 2 minutes, until the bottom is lightly browned. Flip the omelet over and cook for 2 to 3 minutes more, until the other side is lightly browned and the cheese is melted. Slide the omelet onto a plate and cut in half to serve.

SWAP IT: This recipe offers just one example of how to use leftover meat, vegetables, or even sauces you have on hand. Get creative and prevent waste by tossing whatever you have available into this dish!

Per Serving: Calories: 506; Total fat: 41g; Total carbs: 8g; Protein: 28g; Fiber: 2g; Sugar: 3g; Sodium: 685mg

MEDITERRANEAN BREAKFAST PITAS

SUPER QUICK, VEGETARIAN
PREP TIME: 10 MINUTES / COOK TIME: 5 MINUTES

If you're looking for a new, easy breakfast idea to add to your repertoire, look no further than these simple and portable breakfast pitas. You know when all of the ingredients taste delicious on their own they're really going to be scrumptious when combined.

3 large eggs

2 tablespoons milk

Salt

1 tablespoon unsalted butter, divided

2 cups spinach

1 whole-wheat pita, halved

2 tablespoons crumbled feta cheese

½ medium avocado, pitted, scooped, and sliced

1. In a small bowl, beat the eggs and milk and season with salt.

2. In a medium skillet over medium-high heat, melt ½ tablespoon of the butter until it becomes foamy. Add the egg mixture and cook, stirring occasionally, until the eggs are fully cooked through, about 3 minutes. Set aside.

3. Melt the remaining ½ tablespoon of butter in the skillet. Add the spinach and cook for 1 to 2 minutes, until wilted. Season with salt. Set aside.

4. Place half of the egg mixture and spinach into each of the pita halves, and top with the feta cheese and avocado slices. Plate and serve.

Per Serving: Calories: 355; Total fat: 23g; Total carbs: 24g; Protein: 16g; Fiber: 6g; Sugar: 2g; Sodium: 463mg

NORWEGIAN EGGS BENEDICT

SUPER QUICK
PREP TIME: 5 MINUTES / COOK TIME: 10 MINUTES

To me, there is nothing more satisfying than the creaminess of a poached egg paired with the saltiness of smoked salmon and capers. This hearty brunch recipe can be enjoyed anytime—what's better than breakfast for dinner?

4 cups water

1 tablespoon white vinegar

2 large eggs

½ cup arugula

4 smoked salmon slices

2 brioche slices, toasted

1 teaspoon capers

Freshly ground
   black pepper

1. In a medium pot, bring the water to a simmer. Add the vinegar, which will help set the eggs more quickly.

2. Gently crack the eggs into a bowl without breaking the yolks. Slowly pour the eggs, one at a time, into the water; simmer until the egg whites turn white, approximately 2 minutes. Using a slotted spoon, gently remove the eggs from the water, and place them on paper towels to drain.

3. Place ¼ cup of arugula, 2 slices of smoked salmon, and 1 egg on each slice of toast. Top with ½ teaspoon of capers on each slice and sprinkle with pepper. Serve while the eggs are hot.

SWAP IT: Replace the brioche with bagels, baguette slices, or your favorite toast.

Per Serving: Calories: 341; Total fat: 10g; Total carbs: 37g; Protein: 23g; Fiber: 2g; Sugar: 5g; Sodium: 1586mg

POTATO-LEEK FRITTATA

5-INGREDIENT, GLUTEN-FREE, VEGETARIAN
PREP TIME: 10 MINUTES / COOK TIME: 25 MINUTES

This recipe is my go-to for weekend brunch. I absolutely love the combination of potatoes and leeks, which add a delicately sweet onion flavor. Let the overhanging edges of the crust get a bit crispy—they are worth fighting over!

1 tablespoon
 unsalted butter

½ cup leeks, halved
 lengthwise, rinsed well,
 and thinly sliced

1 medium russet potato,
 cubed or shredded

Salt

Freshly ground
 black pepper

4 large eggs, lightly beaten

½ cup extra-sharp cheddar
 cheese, grated

1. Melt the butter in an oven-safe skillet over medium-low heat. Add the leeks and potato, and cook for 10 to 15 minutes, until softened. Season with salt and pepper.

2. Preheat the oven to 400°F.

3. In a medium bowl, combine the eggs and cheddar cheese. Pour the egg mixture over the potatoes and leeks and cook over medium-low heat, until the eggs are almost set, 8 to 10 minutes. Transfer the skillet to the oven and bake about 10 minutes more, until the eggs are set and cheese is browned. Serve warm.

ADD IT: Boost the color and nutritional value by adding in some dark leafy greens, such as spinach, kale, or chard, to this frittata. Sauté the greens with the potatoes and leeks during the last 2 minutes of cook time to bring out their flavor.

Per Serving: Calories: 402; Total fat: 25g; Total carbs: 23g; Protein: 22g; Fiber: 3g; Sugar: 3g; Sodium: 404mg

BREAKFAST NAAN PIZZA

COMFORT FOOD
PREP TIME: 10 MINUTES / COOK TIME: 40 MINUTES

Everything about this breakfast naan pizza is perfection. The crispy, crumbly bacon, mild cheese, spicy jalapeño peppers, and fresh parsley and scallions make this flatbread an excellent way to kick-start the day.

4 bacon slices

2 naan pieces

½ cup grated
  Parmesan cheese

½ cup shredded
  mozzarella cheese

3 jalapeño peppers, sliced

2 eggs

Salt

Freshly ground
  black pepper

1 tablespoon finely
  chopped fresh flat-leaf
  parsley, for garnish

1 tablespoon thinly sliced
  scallions, for garnish

1. Preheat the oven to 400°F.

2. Place the bacon in a single layer on a baking sheet. Bake for 20 to 25 minutes, or until crisp. Remove the bacon and let it cool on a paper towel–lined plate. Drain the fat from the baking sheet and wipe the pan clean with a paper towel. Once the bacon has cooled, break into pieces.

3. Place the naan on the baking sheet, and top each piece with half the parmesan and mozzarella cheeses, bacon, and jalapeño peppers. Gently crack an egg over the top of each pizza and season with salt and pepper.

4. Bake for 10 to 12 minutes, or until the eggs are set but the yolks are still runny. Garnish with parsley and scallions, and enjoy.

SWAP IT: This recipe also works well with pita bread if you can't find naan.

Per Serving: Calories: 698; Total fat: 38g; Total carbs: 48g;
Protein: 42g; Fiber: 3g; Sugar: 1g; Sodium: 1668mg

ROASTED POTATO HASH

GLUTEN-FREE, VEGETARIAN
PREP TIME: 15 MINUTES / COOK TIME: 25 MINUTES

Is there anything better than a hearty breakfast of crispy potatoes? This hash reminds me of the potatoes you get at a diner. You can just eat the hash alone (no judgment here), or top with a fried egg for some protein.

1 tablespoon unsalted butter, divided

3 garlic cloves, thinly sliced

⅓ cup diced onion

⅓ cup diced red bell pepper

2 cups diced Yukon Gold potatoes

1 tablespoon extra-virgin olive oil

2 thyme sprigs, whole or leaves chopped, stems discarded

2 rosemary sprigs, whole or leaves chopped, stems discarded

Salt

Freshly ground black pepper

1 tablespoon finely chopped fresh chives (optional)

1. Melt ½ tablespoon of the butter in a Dutch oven over medium heat.

2. Add the garlic and onion and cook, stirring often, for 3 to 5 minutes. Remove the garlic and onion and set aside.

3. Add the bell pepper to the Dutch oven and cook for 2 to 3 minutes. Sprinkle with salt. Remove and set aside.

4. In a medium bowl, toss the potatoes with the olive oil.

5. Increase the heat to medium-high and melt the remaining ½ tablespoon of butter in the Dutch oven. Add the potatoes, thyme, and rosemary, cover, and cook for 20 minutes, stirring only once or twice to allow the potatoes to develop crisp brown edges. Sprinkle with salt.

6. Add the garlic, onion, and bell pepper to the potatoes and season with pepper. Toss to combine. Remove any herb sprigs if they are left whole. Divide the hash between 2 plates, and garnish with fresh chives (if using).

SWAP IT: Instead of Yukon potatoes, try sweet potatoes for an extra dose of beta-carotene and vitamin C to start your day!

Per Serving: Calories: 235; Total fat: 13g; Total carbs: 28g; Protein: 3g; Fiber: 4g; Sugar: 4g; Sodium: 129mg

serves
2

BRUSSELS SPROUTS HASH

GLUTEN-FREE
PREP TIME: 15 MINUTES / COOK TIME: 30 MINUTES

Please don't dismiss this recipe just because it has Brussels sprouts! I used to dislike Brussels sprouts in any form—until I tried this dish. These are crispy-good, and with the addition of bacon and eggs, this dish is guaranteed to be a hit with both of you.

4 bacon slices, cut into
   1-inch pieces

1 medium sweet
   potato, diced

2 garlic cloves, minced

2 cups Brussels sprouts,
   trimmed and quartered

1 cup diced red bell pepper

1 tablespoon extra-virgin
   olive oil

Salt

Freshly ground
   black pepper

2 large eggs

Red pepper flakes
   (optional)

1. In a Dutch oven over medium-high heat, cook the bacon until crispy, 6 to 8 minutes. Transfer the bacon to a paper towel–lined plate and crumble it when cool.

2. Turn the heat to medium. Add the sweet potato and garlic to the Dutch oven, and cook for 5 to 7 minutes, stirring occasionally, until soft.

3. Stir in the Brussels sprouts and bell pepper, along with the olive oil. Season generously with salt and pepper. Sauté for 8 to 10 minutes, stirring occasionally, until the Brussels sprouts are bright green and fork-tender.

4. Make two small wells in the hash and crack an egg into each. Cover the Dutch oven and cook until the eggs are set but the yolks are still runny, 3 to 5 minutes.

5. Sprinkle with bacon pieces and red pepper flakes (if using) and serve.

PREP HACK: Cut up the Brussels sprouts, red bell pepper, and sweet potato ahead of time, and refrigerate them in a glass or BPA-free plastic container until ready to use.

Per Serving: Calories: 450; Total fat: 28g; Total carbs: 26g; Protein: 25g; Fiber: 6g; Sugar: 9g; Sodium: 1070mg

SAUSAGE-STUFFED AVOCADO BOATS

GLUTEN-FREE

PREP TIME: 10 MINUTES / COOK TIME: 30 MINUTES

I'm always on the lookout for easy breakfast recipes that can also work for dinner. You can add a spicy kick to these avocado boats by topping them with jalapeño peppers.

2 large avocados

1 Italian sausage

¼ teaspoon garlic powder

Salt

Freshly ground
black pepper

4 small eggs

½ cup grated
Parmesan cheese

Fresh parsley, finely
chopped, for garnish

2 jalapeño peppers, sliced,
for garnish (optional)

1. Halve the avocados lengthwise and remove the pits. Using a spoon, scoop out a small amount of the avocado flesh, leaving about ¼ inch on the sides within the peel, creating "cups." Dice up the flesh you removed into small cubes, and set aside.

2. Place the raw sausage link on the work surface. Using the tip of a knife, slice lengthwise through the sausage casing. Peel away the casing and turn the filling out into a bowl. Add the garlic powder and season with salt and pepper. Mix until well combined, breaking up the sausage.

3. Add in the diced avocado, tossing gently. Scoop the mixture into each of the avocado cups. There should be some room on top.

4. Crack an egg on top of the mixture in each of the cups. Sprinkle with the Parmesan cheese.

5. Pour 1 cup of water into the electric pressure cooker and place a trivet or iron tripod inside. Set the avocado cups on the trivet. Cover, and cook on high pressure for 20 minutes. Once done, let the pressure release naturally, about 10 minutes.

6. Turn off the cooker, open the lid, and remove the avocado cups from the pot. Garnish with fresh parsley and jalapeño peppers (if using) and serve.

Per Serving: Calories: 496; Total fat: 40g; Total carbs: 17g; Protein: 24g; Fiber: 12g; Sugar: 1g; Sodium: 643mg

TATER TOT CASSEROLE

COMFORT FOOD, GLUTEN-FREE
PREP TIME: 10 MINUTES / COOK TIME: 30 MINUTES

If you want to know what you should make with tater tots, I have the answer. This savory potato, spinach, and sausage casserole screams comfort food.

1 garlic clove, minced

1 cup milk

1 large egg

¼ teaspoon dried thyme

Salt

3 Italian sausages, sliced ½-inch thick

2 cups spinach

1 cup grated cheddar cheese

12 ounces frozen tater tots

1. Preheat the oven to 350°F.

2. In a medium bowl, combine the garlic, milk, egg, and thyme, and season with salt. Mix well. Add the sausage and spinach, stirring to combine. Pour the mixture into a casserole dish.

3. Sprinkle the casserole with the cheddar cheese and line the tater tots on top.

4. Bake in the oven for 25 to 30 minutes, or until the cheese is bubbly and the tater tots are cooked through. Serve warm.

> **PREP HACK:** Prep this casserole the night before by following steps 2 and 3, store overnight in the fridge, then proceed with baking the next day. Or you can prepare it ahead of time and freeze for up to two weeks. Thaw in the fridge overnight. Let it sit out at room temperature 30 minutes before baking.

Per Serving: Calories: 969; Total fat: 68g; Total carbs: 49g; Protein: 39g; Fiber: 5g; Sugar: 7g; Sodium: 1871mg

TUNA CROISSANTS

COMFORT FOOD
PREP TIME: 10 MINUTES / COOK TIME: 20 MINUTES

These umami-flavored tuna croissants are not just great for breakfast—they're also the perfect appetizer for your next party. Keep any leftovers in a sealed container, and toast them the next day.

1 (5-ounce) can
   albacore tuna

1½ teaspoons white
   miso paste

1 teaspoon ginger paste

½ teaspoon wasabi paste

1 teaspoon light soy sauce

8 dried nori
   (seaweed) snacks

1 (8-ounce) package
   crescent roll dough,
   original

1 egg yolk, beaten

3 tablespoons
   sesame seeds

1. Preheat the oven to 375°F.

2. Line a baking sheet with parchment paper.

3. In a small bowl, combine the tuna, miso paste, ginger paste, wasabi paste, and soy sauce. Mix well.

4. On a clean surface, place 1 nori sheet on top of each piece of crescent roll dough. Add 1 teaspoon of the tuna mixture on top and roll up, starting from the wide end to the point.

5. Arrange the croissants on the prepared baking sheet. Brush the tops of the rolls with egg yolk and sprinkle the rolls with the sesame seeds.

6. Bake until puffed and golden brown, 18 to 20 minutes. Let cool on a wire rack for 2 to 3 minutes before serving.

SWAP IT: Instead of sesame seeds, you can use furikake for a sweet and salty flavor. This is a dry Japanese seasoning, typically consisting of a mixture of dried and ground fish, sesame seeds, chopped seaweed, sugar, and salt. You can find it in the Asian food aisle.

Per Serving: Calories: 650; Total fat: 34g; Total carbs: 50g; Protein: 30g; Fiber: 4g; Sugar: 8g; Sodium: 1000mg

slow
cooker

serves
2

SLOW COOKER CINNAMON ROLLS

COMFORT FOOD, VEGETARIAN

WITH LEFTOVERS / PREP TIME: 10 MINUTES / COOK TIME: 2 HOURS

I love spending time in the kitchen, but sometimes I just want something more hands-off. Luckily, these cinnamon rolls can be done in a slow cooker while I cozy up in bed.

¼ cup brown sugar

½ teaspoon cinnamon

1½ cups all-purpose flour

3 tablespoons granulated sugar

½ teaspoon baking powder

Pinch salt

½ cup milk

½ cup (1 stick) butter, melted and divided, plus 2 tablespoons, softened

1 tablespoon apple cider vinegar

1. In a small bowl, combine the brown sugar and cinnamon and set aside.

2. In a medium mixing bowl, whisk the flour with the granulated sugar, baking powder, and salt.

3. In a small cup, combine the milk, ¼ cup of the melted butter, and the apple cider vinegar.

4. Add the milk mixture to the flour mixture, and mix until the dough just starts to come together. Add in the remaining ¼ cup melted butter and mix until all of the flour is incorporated and the dough is no longer sticky.

5. Turn the dough out onto a floured work surface and roll into a ¼-inch-thick rectangle. Dot the softened butter on top, then sprinkle with cinnamon and sugar. Starting from a long side, roll the dough around the filling to form a log; cut into 4 rolls.

6. Spray the slow cooker with nonstick cooking spray. Place the cinnamon dough pieces inside. Cover and cook on high for 2 hours, checking every 30 minutes to make sure the edges and bottom are not burning. Turn off the slow cooker, and let it sit for 5 minutes. Serve warm.

Per Serving: Calories: 1063; Total fat: 60g; Total carbs: 120g; Protein: 14g; Fiber: 3g; Sugar: 39g; Sodium: 123mg

BANANA AND CHOCOLATE PASTRIES

SUPER QUICK, 5-INGREDIENT, COMFORT FOOD, VEGETARIAN
PREP TIME: 10 MINUTES / COOK TIME: 15 MINUTES

sheet pan

serves
2

If I could stockpile one food, it would be these banana and chocolate pastries. Flaky puff pastry, bananas, sweet mascarpone, and chocolate are an irresistible combination. I make this quick dessert-for-breakfast when I really want to treat myself. I sometimes add a drizzle of melted chocolate on top, because who doesn't love chocolate?

1 frozen puff pastry sheet, thawed, but still cold

Flour, for dusting

1 cup mascarpone cheese

½ cup chopped dark chocolate

2 medium ripe bananas, halved lengthwise

Confectioners' sugar (optional)

1. Preheat the oven to 400°F.

2. Line a baking sheet with parchment paper or a nonstick baking mat.

3. Unfold the puff pastry onto a lightly floured work surface. Spread the mascarpone cheese on top of the pastry, and sprinkle with dark chocolate. Add the bananas along the long edge of the pastry border. Starting at the long end with the bananas, roll up tightly to make a log.

4. Bake for 15 minutes, or until puffed and golden. Cut into 6 slices and sprinkle with confectioners' sugar (if using) before serving. Store in an airtight container at room temperature to keep the pastry crispy.

Per Serving: Calories: 964; Total fat: 69g; Total carbs: 85g; Protein: 13g; Fiber: 6g; Sugar: 29g; Sodium: 257mg

FRENCH TOAST CASSEROLE

COMFORT FOOD, VEGETARIAN
PREP TIME: 10 MINUTES / COOK TIME: 30 MINUTES

Who loves brunch? Trick question—EVERYONE loves brunch! The only problem with it is having to get up super early to cook everything, so I'm always looking for dishes I can make quickly, or even prep the night before. This casserole, a decadent meal that rewards the senses with the flavors of cinnamon, pecans, and confectioners' sugar, fits the bill. If you can't find challah, you can use Italian or brioche bread.

1 cup milk

2 large eggs

1 teaspoon vanilla extract

1 tablespoon light brown sugar

1 teaspoon cinnamon

4 challah bread slices, ripped into chunks

½ cup chopped pecans

1 teaspoon confectioners' sugar, for dusting

½ cup maple syrup, for serving

1. Preheat the oven to 375°F.

2. Lightly grease a casserole dish.

3. In a medium bowl, whisk together the milk, eggs, and vanilla. Set aside.

4. In a small bowl, combine the brown sugar and cinnamon.

5. Arrange the bread slices in the prepared casserole dish. Pour the egg mixture on top and sprinkle with the brown sugar mixture and pecans. Lightly press the bread into the egg wash to ensure the bread slices are evenly soaked.

6. Bake for 30 minutes, or until the center is cooked through and the top is golden brown. Let it cool.

7. Dust with the confectioners' sugar and serve with maple syrup.

PREP HACK: To make this casserole the night before, simply follow steps 2 through 5, then cover and refrigerate overnight. In the morning, let the dish warm up on the counter as your oven preheats, and continue with steps 6 and 7. You can also freeze uncooked French toast casserole for up to 2 months. Thaw in the fridge overnight and then bake as directed.

Per Serving: Calories: 825; Total fat: 37g; Total carbs: 104g; Protein: 19g; Fiber: 5g; Sugar: 64g; Sodium: 345mg

Soups and Salads

FRENCH ONION MUSHROOM SOUP

VEGETARIAN
PREP TIME: 15 MINUTES / COOK TIME: 50 MINUTES

The best thing about this comforting dish is it delivers a delicious and satisfying everyday meal with only a little prep time. This rich onion and mushroom soup topped with perfectly crunchy and cheesy toasts could be your new family favorite.

1 tablespoon
  unsalted butter

1 tablespoon extra-virgin
  olive oil

1 medium sweet onion,
  thinly sliced

2 cups thinly sliced cremini
  mushrooms

1 cup asparagus, cut into
  1-inch sections

2 dried thyme sprigs

4 cups vegetable stock

½ cup dry white wine

Salt

Freshly ground
  black pepper

2 or 4 (¾-inch-thick) French
  baguette slices

¼ cup shredded or grated
  Gruyère cheese

¼ cup shredded
  Swiss cheese

1. Preheat the oven to broil.

2. In a Dutch oven over medium heat, melt the butter and heat the olive oil. Add the onion and cook, stirring occasionally, for about 30 minutes, or until the onion turns deep golden brown and is caramelized.

3. Add the mushrooms, asparagus, and thyme. Cook, stirring occasionally, for 5 minutes.

4. Pour in the stock and wine, and bring to a boil. Reduce heat to low and simmer, stirring occasionally, until the liquid is slightly reduced, 15 to 20 minutes. Remove the thyme and discard. Season with salt and pepper.

5. Place the baguette slices over the soup to cover the surface completely; top with the Gruyère and Swiss cheeses. Place the Dutch oven in the oven and broil until the cheeses have melted and the baguettes are browned, 2 to 4 minutes. Serve immediately.

SWAP IT: Instead of dry white wine, you can use ½ cup of sherry, or just use more broth.

Per Serving: Calories: 435; Total fat: 25g; Total carbs: 36g; Protein: 15g; Fiber: 4g; Sugar: 11g; Sodium: 415mg

CURRIED PUMPKIN SOUP

SUPER QUICK, GLUTEN-FREE, VEGAN
PREP TIME: 5 MINUTES / COOK TIME: 15 MINUTES

Nowadays, I find myself making pumpkin soup more, thanks to the electric pressure cooker. It comes out perfectly every time, and there's no babysitting needed. However, you can also make it the standard way on the stovetop. Either way, it's delicious!

1 tablespoon extra-virgin olive oil

½ cup diced onion

2 tablespoons red curry paste

1 (15-ounce) can pumpkin purée

4 cups vegetable stock

1 cup coconut milk

2 teaspoons freshly squeezed lime juice

Salt

1 tablespoon fresh cilantro, chopped, for garnish

1. Press the sauté mode button on the electric pressure cooker and heat the oil. Add the onion, and sauté for 3 minutes.

2. Add the curry paste, pumpkin purée, and stock, and stir to combine.

3. Cover, and cook at high pressure for 8 minutes. When done, let the pressure release naturally, about 10 minutes.

4. Turn off the cooker and open the lid. Stir in the coconut milk, lime juice, and salt, to taste, until well combined. Garnish with cilantro and serve.

COOKING TIP: This recipe can also be done on the stove. Add the oil and onion to a heated pot or Dutch oven, then sauté for 5 minutes over medium-high heat. Add the curry paste, purée, and stock, and stir to combine. Reduce the heat to low and let simmer until slightly thickened, about 15 minutes. Add the coconut milk, lime juice, and salt. Stir well. Divide between 2 bowls and garnish with cilantro.

Per Serving: Calories: 545; Total fat: 49g; Total carbs: 37g; Protein: 6g; Fiber: 10g; Sugar: 17g; Sodium: 548mg

slow
cooker

serves
2

BROCCOLI CHEDDAR SOUP

GLUTEN-FREE
PREP TIME: 15 MINUTES / COOK TIME: 4 HOURS

This filling and comforting broccoli cheddar soup makes dinner as easy as can be. Place everything in your slow cooker and turn it on at lunchtime—you'll have a simple and delicious soup by the time you're ready for dinner, without too much effort.

1 tablespoon
  unsalted butter

1 cup diced onion

1 cup coarsely chopped
  broccoli florets

1 cup matchstick-cut
  carrots

½ cup thinly sliced celery

2 cups chicken stock

1 cup evaporated milk

Salt

Freshly ground
  black pepper

½ cup shredded
  cheddar cheese

1. Turn the slow cooker to high. Heat the butter in the cooker and add the onion. Cook, stirring continuously, for 3 to 5 minutes, or until the onions are tender.

2. Add the broccoli, carrots, celery, stock, and milk to the slow cooker and season with salt and pepper. Cover the cooker with the lid and cook on low for 3 to 4 hours, or until the broccoli is tender.

3. Add the cheddar cheese and stir until it is melted. Serve warm.

SWAP IT: Although I prefer to use a cheddar cheese for this soup, you can substitute almost any shredded mild cheese, such as Colby Jack.

Per Serving: Calories: 411; Total fat: 26g; Total carbs: 29g; Protein: 19g; Fiber: 4g; Sugar: 20g; Sodium: 542mg

QUINOA VEGETABLE SOUP

GLUTEN-FREE, VEGAN
PREP TIME: 15 MINUTES / COOK TIME: 25 MINUTES

This soup is on the regular rotation at our house for Meatless Mondays. Not only is it easy to make, it's also packed with nutrients and totally customizable. And no matter what vegetables you include, you can feel good that the base is quinoa, a complete protein packed with fiber and one of the few plant foods containing all nine of the essential amino acids.

1 tablespoon extra-virgin olive oil

1 garlic clove, minced

1 carrot, peeled and diced

Salt

Freshly ground black pepper

1 (28-ounce) can diced tomatoes

1 (15.5-ounce) can cannellini beans, drained and rinsed

½ cup quinoa

6 cups vegetable stock

1 tablespoon gluten-free soy sauce

2 cups thinly sliced Tuscan kale leaves

Red pepper flakes, for garnish (optional)

1. Heat the oil in a pot over medium-high heat. Add the garlic and carrot, and season with salt and pepper. Cook, stirring occasionally, until the vegetables are soft, about 10 minutes.

2. Add the tomatoes, beans, and quinoa. Pour in the stock and stir to combine. Bring to a boil and cook until the quinoa is tender, about 10 minutes. Stir in the soy sauce.

3. Stir in the kale and cook 2 to 3 minutes, until wilted. Season with salt and pepper, and red pepper flakes (if using), and serve.

Per Serving: Calories: 561; Total fat: 11g; Total carbs: 96g; Protein: 25g; Fiber: 24g; Sugar: 25g; Sodium: 1516mg

SUN-DRIED TOMATO TORTELLINI SOUP

COMFORT FOOD
PREP TIME: 10 MINUTES / COOK TIME: 30 MINUTES

If you are looking for a comforting soup recipe, this is it. Oh my goodness—garlic and Parmesan cheese make this creamy tomato soup special enough for a celebratory night at home.

1 tablespoon extra-virgin olive oil

1 garlic clove, minced

¼ cup chopped sun-dried tomatoes

½ tablespoon tomato paste

½ cup diced onion

2 cups chicken stock

1 cup heavy cream

½ tablespoon Italian seasoning

Salt

Freshly ground black pepper

9 ounces fresh or frozen three-cheese tortellini

1 cup spinach

¼ cup grated Parmesan cheese, for garnish

1. Heat the oil in a pot over medium heat. Add the garlic and cook for 2 minutes. Add the tomatoes, tomato paste, and onion and sauté until tender, 3 to 4 minutes.

2. Add the stock, heavy cream, Italian seasoning, and salt and pepper to taste. Bring to a boil, reduce heat, and simmer for 15 minutes.

3. Add the tortellini and spinach and cook for 3 to 4 minutes if using fresh tortellini, or 7 to 8 minutes for frozen.

4. Garnish with Parmesan cheese and serve immediately.

SWAP IT: To make it vegetarian, use vegetable stock instead of the chicken stock—none of the delicious flavor will be lost with the swap!

Per Serving: Calories: 982; Total fat: 68g; Total carbs: 74g; Protein: 25g; Fiber: 1g; Sugar: 3g; Sodium: 734mg

SPICY CLAM AND CORN CHOWDER

COMFORT FOOD, GLUTEN-FREE
PREP TIME: 15 MINUTES / COOK TIME: 25 MINUTES

This chowder keeps me warm on cold rainy days and is also my new favorite summer soup. It's creamy, yet light, spicy, and packed with delicious sweet corn and clams. Plus, everything tastes better with bacon!

4 bacon slices, chopped

1 large russet potato, cut into 1-inch pieces

2 tablespoons seafood seasoning, such as Old Bay

2 bay leaves

2 garlic cloves, chopped

¼ cup finely chopped jalapeño peppers

5 cups chicken stock

1 cup heavy cream

½ cup chopped clams, canned or fresh, cleaned

2 cups frozen corn kernels, thawed

Salt

Freshly ground black pepper

1. Cook the bacon in a Dutch oven over low heat until crispy, about 10 minutes. Using a slotted spoon, remove the bacon and set aside, reserving the bacon grease in the pot.

2. Add the potato and cook, stirring occasionally, for 6 to 8 minutes, or until tender.

3. Add the seafood seasoning, bay leaves, garlic, and jalapeño peppers, and cook, stirring occasionally, for 3 to 5 minutes.

4. Stir in the stock and heavy cream. Add the clams and corn, and stir to combine. Season with salt and pepper. Remove the bay leaves.

5. To serve, ladle into individual serving bowls. Crumble the bacon and sprinkle over the top before serving.

SWAP IT: For a richer flavor, try using fish broth instead of chicken stock, and add ½ cup of dry white wine to step 4.

Per Serving: Calories: 719; Total fat: 41g; Total carbs: 53g; Protein: 38g; Fiber: 6g; Sugar: 6g; Sodium: 2140mg

CHICKEN BARLEY SOUP

COMFORT FOOD
PREP TIME: 15 MINUTES / COOK TIME: 4 HOURS

I first tried this soup when I visited Israel, and it was so good I had to re-create it at home. The aroma of chicken, barley, and vegetables simmering in a savory broth will have your mouth watering. Pair this soup with some crusty bread.

1 cup chopped carrot

1 cup chopped celery

1 cup chopped onion

2 (3- to 4-ounce) boneless, skinless chicken breasts, cut into ½-inch pieces

6 cups chicken stock

1 cup quick-cooking barley

5 thyme sprigs

Salt

Freshly ground black pepper

1. In a slow cooker, add the carrot, celery, onion, chicken, stock, barley, thyme, and season with salt and pepper. Stir and cover.

2. Cook on low for 4 hours, until the barley is cooked through. Remove the thyme sprigs before serving.

SWAP IT: This soup is versatile: Use cooked chicken or turkey meat, or raw chicken thighs.

Per Serving: Calories: 393; Total fat: 3g; Total carbs: 54g; Protein: 39g; Fiber: 9g; Sugar: 6g; Sodium: 447mg

SAUSAGE AND LENTIL SOUP

COMFORT FOOD, GLUTEN-FREE
WITH LEFTOVERS / PREP TIME: 15 MINUTES / COOK TIME: 30 MINUTES

This lentil soup is one of the best soups I've ever made—and because of the electric pressure cooker, it's also one of the easiest. Packed with protein, fiber, and vitamins, this thick and hearty soup is a well-rounded meal in a bowl. This recipe makes a little more than two bowls, but you'll be glad you have some extra for the next day.

1 tablespoon extra-virgin olive oil

2 hot or sweet Italian sausages, casings removed

1 garlic clove, minced

1 cup diced onion

1 cup diced celery

2 cups dried lentils

4 cups chicken stock

1 (15-ounce) can diced tomatoes

1 rosemary sprig

2 fresh bay leaves

2 cups baby kale leaves, loosely packed

Salt

Freshly ground black pepper

1. Turn the electric pressure cooker on sauté mode. Add the olive oil, sausage, and garlic. Break the sausage into crumbles and cook for 5 minutes, or until browned. Add the onion and celery, and sauté for 3 minutes more.

2. Add the lentils and stir to combine.

3. Add the stock, diced tomatoes, rosemary, and bay leaves.

4. Cover, and cook on high pressure for 10 minutes. Once done, allow the pressure to release naturally, about 10 minutes.

5. Turn off the pot, and open the lid. Add the kale, and stir to combine. Season with salt and pepper, and remove the bay leaves before serving.

COOKING TIP: To prepare in a pot or Dutch oven, heat the olive oil and garlic, then cook the sausage, onion, celery, and lentils as directed. Cover and simmer the stock, tomatoes, rosemary, and bay leaves on low until the lentils are tender, 25 to 30 minutes. Stir in the kale, cook until wilted, then season with salt and pepper.

Per Serving: Calories: 1030; Total fat: 24g; Total carbs: 140g; Protein: 65g; Fiber: 64g; Sugar: 13g; Sodium: 644mg

ITALIAN MEATBALL SOUP

SUPER QUICK, COMFORT FOOD
PREP TIME: 10 MINUTES / COOK TIME: 10 MINUTES

I have a bit of an obsession with meatball soup. This soul-soothing soup flavored with Tuscan herbs jumps to the top of my favorites list during the fall. Italian sausage and hearty kale always make a good duo, but if you don't have access to Italian sausage meatballs, any frozen meatballs will suffice.

1 tablespoon extra-virgin olive oil

2 garlic cloves, finely minced

1 cup diced onion

1 tablespoon Italian seasoning

4 cups chicken stock

1 (8-ounce) bag frozen cooked Italian sausage meatballs, thawed

1 (15.5-ounce) can cannellini beans, drained and rinsed

1 cup orzo pasta

2 cups spinach

Salt

⅓ cup grated Parmesan cheese

1. Turn the electric pressure cooker on sauté mode. Add the olive oil, garlic, and onion, and cook for 3 minutes, until onions are soft.

2. Add the Italian seasoning, stock, meatballs, beans, and pasta. Cover, and cook on high pressure for 10 minutes. Allow the pressure to release naturally, about 10 minutes.

3. Open the lid, add the spinach, and stir. Let the soup sit for 5 minutes so the pasta is fully cooked and the spinach is wilted. Season with salt and top with Parmesan cheese before serving.

COOKING TIP: To make this dish in a pot or Dutch oven, cook the olive oil, garlic, and onion for 4 minutes, or until the onion is soft. Add the Italian seasoning, stock, meatballs, beans, and pasta, bring to a boil, and simmer for 10 minutes. Add the spinach and cook for 2 minutes. Sprinkle with salt and Parmesan cheese.

Per Serving: Calories: 831; Total fat: 36g; Total carbs: 79g; Protein: 46g; Fiber: 15g; Sugar: 9g; Sodium: 1644mg

ROASTED TOMATO SALAD

SUPER QUICK, GLUTEN-FREE, VEGETARIAN
PREP TIME: 10 MINUTES / COOK TIME: 20 MINUTES

When sweet tomatoes are in season, this salad climbs to the top of my favorites list. The spiciness of the arugula provides a nice counterbalance to the sweetness of the tomatoes.

2 garlic cloves,
  finely minced

1 tablespoon freshly
  squeezed lemon juice

1 tablespoon finely
  chopped fresh oregano

3 tablespoons extra-virgin
  olive oil, divided

Salt

2 cups cherry tomatoes

½ small onion, thinly sliced

2 cups arugula

1 tablespoon
  Parmesan cheese

1. Preheat the oven to 400°F.

2. In a small bowl, combine the garlic, lemon juice, oregano, 2 tablespoons of olive oil, and season with salt. Set aside.

3. Spread the tomatoes and onion on a baking sheet. Drizzle with the remaining 1 tablespoon of olive oil and sprinkle with salt. Roast until the tomatoes and onion are soft, 15 to 20 minutes. Set aside to cool.

4. Divide the arugula between two plates. Add the tomatoes and onion on top, and drizzle with the dressing. Sprinkle with Parmesan cheese, and serve.

COOKING TIP: To lessen the bitterness of the arugula, marinate the greens in a mixture of 1 tablespoon of olive oil and lemon juice for at least 30 minutes. Massage the arugula greens with your hands every few minutes to deepen the wilting process. When they're ready, your wilted greens will be fresh, tangy, and full of flavor!

Per Serving: Calories: 253; Total fat: 23g; Total carbs: 13g; Protein: 4g; Fiber: 4g; Sugar: 7g; Sodium: 128mg

ROASTED CHICKPEA AND
GREEN BEAN SALAD

SUPER QUICK, GLUTEN-FREE, VEGAN
PREP TIME: 10 MINUTES / COOK TIME: 25 MINUTES

Ripe juicy tomatoes tossed with olive oil, lemon juice, and fresh herbs makes for a salad that can't be beat on a summer day—unless it's topped with roasted chickpeas and green beans. The roasting process intensifies the flavors and adds crunch to this delectable duo.

1 cup green beans,
  ends trimmed

2 cups canned chickpeas
  (garbanzo beans),
  drained and rinsed

3 tablespoons extra-virgin
  olive oil, divided

Salt

Freshly ground
  black pepper

2 large tomatoes,
  quartered

1 tablespoon chopped
  fresh parsley

1 tablespoon chopped
  fresh basil

1 teaspoon
  smoked paprika

2 tablespoons freshly
  squeezed lemon juice

1. Preheat the oven to 400°F.

2. Toss the green beans and chickpeas with 2 tablespoons of olive oil, and season with salt and pepper. Spread them out on a sheet pan, and bake for 25 minutes, stirring occasionally, or until the chickpeas are crisp and the green beans are tender and lightly browned.

3. In a large bowl, mix together tomatoes, parsley, basil, the remaining 1 tablespoon of olive oil, paprika, and lemon juice. Season generously with salt and pepper. Divide the mixture onto 2 plates, top each with half of the roasted chickpea and green bean mixture, and serve immediately.

Per Serving: Calories: 524; Total fat: 25g; Total carbs: 66g; Protein: 15g; Fiber: 15g; Sugar: 6g; Sodium: 812mg

ROASTED RED PEPPER SALAD

GLUTEN-FREE, VEGAN
PREP TIME: 5 MINUTES / COOK TIME: 40 MINUTES

Roasting brings out the sweetness of bell peppers and yields the perfect blend of crispy exterior and juicy interior. In this recipe, roasted red bell peppers serve as a warm base for a refreshing salad of corn and cucumber, adorned with a tasty vinaigrette dressing.

2 medium red bell peppers

1 tablespoon
  balsamic vinegar

½ tablespoon
  whole-grain mustard

2 tablespoons extra-virgin
  olive oil, plus more for
  drizzling

Salt

1 cup fresh or frozen corn
  kernels, thawed

1 cup diced cucumber

Fresh basil leaves, roughly
  chopped, for serving

1. Turn the broiler to high and place the oven rack in the top position. Place the bell peppers on a foil-lined rimmed baking sheet. Broil the peppers until the skins blister, about 5 minutes.

2. With tongs, rotate the peppers a quarter turn. Continue to broil and rotate until the peppers are charred on all sides and tender. Transfer the peppers to a bowl, cover tightly with plastic wrap, and let steam for 20 minutes.

3. Peel and discard the charred skins. Remove the stems and seeds, then cut the peppers into thin strips.

4. In a small bowl, combine the vinegar, mustard, and oil, and season with salt.

5. Arrange the peppers on a plate. Add the corn and cucumber, then drizzle with the vinaigrette and sprinkle with basil before serving.

> **PREP HACK:** To save time, you can use roasted red peppers from a jar, but homemade roasted peppers are more colorful and flavorful.

Per Serving: Calories: 235; Total fat: 15g; Total carbs: 27g; Protein: 4g; Fiber: 4g; Sugar: 9g; Sodium: 113mg

CRISPY EGGPLANT SALAD WITH HALLOUMI CHEESE

SUPER QUICK, COMFORT FOOD, VEGETARIAN
PREP TIME: 15 MINUTES / COOK TIME: 15 MINUTES

If eggplant salad isn't a go-to dish in your house, I encourage you to put it on the list! Throw some sliced eggplant and halloumi cheese on the grill or in a pan, and add it to a bed of fresh greens for a meatless entrée you'll love. This dish can be served hot or chilled. As a cold salad, it offers an excellent make-ahead option.

FOR THE SALAD

4 ounces halloumi, cut into ⅓- to ½-inch-thick slices

2 tablespoons vegetable oil, for frying

1 small eggplant, cut into 1-inch-thick slices

2 eggs, beaten

1 cup dry bread crumbs

2 cups salad mix (red butter lettuce, spinach, or other greens of choice)

2 small tomatoes, quartered

1 small cucumber, cut into small wedges

FOR THE DRESSING

3 tablespoons red wine vinegar

1 garlic clove, finely minced

1 tablespoon extra-virgin olive oil

Salt

Freshly ground black pepper

1. To make the salad, heat a nonstick skillet over high heat. Dry the halloumi cheese slices by blotting them with a paper towel. Add the slices to the skillet and cook for 1 to 2 minutes on each side, or until each side develops a deep brown crust, then set aside on a plate. In the same skillet heat the vegetable oil over medium-high heat. Dip the eggplant slices in the eggs, then in the bread crumbs, and place in the hot oil. Fry 2 to 3 minutes on each side, or until golden brown. Drain on paper towels.

2. To make the dressing, in a small bowl, whisk together the vinegar, garlic, olive oil, and season with salt and pepper.

3. To assemble, divide the salad mix between 2 plates. Add the tomatoes, cucumber, halloumi, and fried eggplant. Drizzle with salad dressing and serve.

PREP IT: If you can't find halloumi, provolone (in a block, not pre-sliced) or any other grilling cheese will work as well.

Per Serving: Calories: 780; Total fat: 43g; Total carbs: 72g; Protein: 31g; Fiber: 14g; Sugar: 17g; Sodium: 1162mg

SOBA SALAD

SUPER QUICK
PREP TIME: 15 MINUTES / COOK TIME: 10 MINUTES

Between work, blogging, trying to squeeze in a workout, and making sure I catch up on my favorite Netflix shows, I'm strapped for time on weeknight evenings, so I'm always on the hunt for dinners I can make in 30 minutes or less. This salad takes less than 30 minutes to make from start to finish, and the bold soy and vinegar flavors of the dressing that infuse the crunchy vegetables and soba noodles will impress anyone. I love this dressing so much that I always have it handy in my fridge, so I can dress any salad in a pinch. I use shrimp in this version, but you can top the soba with any leftover protein you might have—grilled chicken, steak, and tofu would all be delicious!

FOR THE DRESSING

1 tablespoon rice
   wine vinegar

¼ cup reduced-sodium
   soy sauce

1 garlic clove, pressed or
   finely minced

2 tablespoons extra-virgin
   olive oil

FOR THE SALAD

½ (8-ounce) package
   soba noodles

8 ounces large shrimp,
   peeled and deveined

2 scallions, thinly sliced

2 tablespoons chopped
   fresh cilantro

1 teaspoon sesame seeds

1 cup edamame, shelled
   and cooked (optional)

1 cup cucumber, seeded
   and cut into matchsticks
   (optional)

1. To make the dressing, in a small bowl, whisk together the vinegar, soy sauce, garlic, and olive oil, and set aside.

2. To make the salad, bring a pot of water to a boil. Add the soba noodles and cook until al dente, about 4 minutes. Drain the noodles and rinse under cold water. Allow to drain and set aside in a large bowl.

3. Add fresh water to the same pot and bring to a boil. Add the shrimp and cook until pink and opaque throughout, about 2 minutes. Transfer the shrimp to the bowl on top of the noodles.

SOBA SALAD Continues

4. Top the shrimp and noodles with the scallions, cilantro, sesame seeds, edamame (if using), and cucumber (if using). Pour the dressing over the salad and serve immediately.

SWAP IT: Soba noodles are thin, light, dried Japanese noodles made with buckwheat flour. You can get them gluten-free, but check the ingredient label to make sure it does not contain flour. If soba is not available, you can replace them with any long, thin whole-wheat noodles, such as spaghetti.

Per Serving: Calories: 448; Total fat: 15g; Total carbs: 51g; Protein: 32g; Fiber: 1g; Sugar: 2g; Sodium: 1660mg

CRISPY KALE AND SHRIMP SALAD

GLUTEN-FREE
PREP TIME: 15 MINUTES / COOK TIME: 35 MINUTES

Need an easy-to-make but impressive appetizer for company on a week-night? Or a healthy dish that doesn't feel like yet another boring salad? Try this dish combining shrimp with crispy kale, crunchy pomegranate seeds, and a zesty lemon dressing. Just wait until you taste this delicious, colorful dish—it's sensory overload.

2 cups kale leaves or baby kale, divided

6 tablespoons extra-virgin olive oil, divided

Salt

Juice and zest of 1 medium lemon, divided

½ teaspoon ground chipotle pepper

12 large shrimp, peeled and deveined

1 teaspoon honey

½ teaspoon Dijon mustard

Freshly ground black pepper

1 tablespoon pomegranate seeds

1. Preheat the oven to 300°F.

2. Spread the kale on a rimmed baking sheet, and drizzle 1 tablespoon of olive oil over top. Season with salt and toss to coat using your hands. Bake for 25 minutes, tossing the kale every 10 minutes.

3. While the kale is baking, in a small bowl, combine 1 tablespoon of the olive oil, lemon zest, chipotle pepper, and season with salt. Add the shrimp, and toss to coat.

4. Remove the baking sheet from the oven and toss the kale. Push the kale to one side of the pan and arrange the shrimp on the other side. Bake until the shrimp turn pink and the kale is crisp, about 10 minutes.

CRISPY KALE AND SHRIMP SALAD Continues

5. In the same small bowl, combine the remaining 4 tablespoons olive oil, lemon juice, honey, and mustard. Whisk until the dressing is well blended. Season with salt and pepper.

6. Divide the salad between 2 plates. Drizzle with the salad dressing, sprinkle with pomegranate seeds, and serve.

ADD IT: For a spicy kick of flavor, add ½ teaspoon of red pepper flakes over this salad.

Per Serving: Calories: 480; Total fat: 42g; Total carbs: 11g; Protein: 20g; Fiber: 1g; Sugar: 3g; Sodium: 416mg

GARLIC ROASTED SHRIMP SALAD

SUPER QUICK, GLUTEN-FREE
PREP TIME: 15 MINUTES / COOK TIME: 10 MINUTES

The pairing of garlic and shrimp is a favorite for many. I make this recipe when I want a light meal I can enjoy while reading a book and unwinding. Light and refreshing, it's elegant enough to serve to guests.

2 garlic cloves, crushed

⅓ cup hot sauce, such as Sriracha or Tabasco

1 tablespoon Worcestershire sauce

1 tablespoon sugar

⅓ cup, plus ¼ cup olive oil, divided

Salt

1 pound large shrimp, peeled and deveined

2 tablespoons freshly squeezed lemon juice, divided

3 cups arugula

1 large English cucumber, chopped

1. Preheat the oven to 450°F.

2. Line a baking sheet with parchment paper.

3. In a small bowl, combine the garlic, hot sauce, Worcestershire sauce, sugar, ⅓ cup of olive oil, and season with salt. Add the shrimp and toss to coat.

4. Place the shrimp on the prepared baking sheet, and roast for 5 to 7 minutes. Set aside and sprinkle with 1 tablespoon of lemon juice.

5. While the shrimp is roasting, place the arugula and cucumber in a bowl. Add the remaining 1 tablespoon of lemon juice, ¼ cup of olive oil, and season with salt. Toss well to coat.

6. Divide the salad between 2 plates and top with shrimp before serving.

ADD IT: In the summer, add 2 cups of watermelon cubes to the greens and serve this salad cold.

Per Serving: Calories: 615; Total fat: 43g; Total carbs: 20g; Protein: 45g; Fiber: 2g; Sugar: 11g; Sodium: 701mg

THAI CHICKEN SALAD

SUPER QUICK, GLUTEN-FREE
PREP TIME: 15 MINUTES / COOK TIME: 15 MINUTES

This salad reminds me of a deconstructed summer roll I had in Thailand. Crunchy with bright, zesty flavors, it's easy to make and easy to clean up after. What more could you want?

3 tablespoons extra-virgin olive oil, divided

1 garlic clove, minced

1 red chile, chopped (optional)

5 ounces ground chicken

2 tablespoons gluten-free soy sauce, divided

2 large eggs

Salt

Freshly ground black pepper

2 tablespoons creamy peanut butter

2 tablespoons water

1 teaspoon brown sugar

1 cup mixed salad greens

2 tablespoons chopped peanuts

2 tablespoons chopped fresh basil, cilantro, or both

4 lime wedges, for garnish (optional)

1. Heat 2 tablespoons of olive oil in a medium skillet over medium-high heat. Add the garlic and chile (if using), and cook, stirring frequently, for 2 to 3 minutes. Add the chicken and cook, stirring to break up any lumps, for 5 minutes, or until cooked through. Add 1 tablespoon of the soy sauce and continue cooking for 1 minute more. Remove the chicken from the skillet and allow to cool slightly in a bowl or on a plate.

2. Add the remaining 1 tablespoon of oil to the hot skillet. Crack the eggs, one at a time, into the skillet. Cook 3 minutes, or until whites are set, flip, and cook 1 minute more. Remove the eggs from the pan and season with salt and pepper.

3. To make the dressing, in a small bowl, combine the peanut butter, remaining 1 tablespoon of soy sauce, water, brown sugar, and season with salt and pepper.

4. To serve, place the mixed greens in a bowl. Add the chicken, peanuts, and chopped herbs. Drizzle with the dressing, toss well, and divide between 2 plates. Top each with a fried egg. Garnish with lime wedges (if using), and serve.

Per Serving: Calories: 461; Total fat: 37g; Total carbs: 10g; Protein: 27g; Fiber: 2g; Sugar: 4g; Sodium: 1200mg

Vegetable Mains

RAINBOW VEGETABLE SKILLET

SUPER QUICK, GLUTEN-FREE, VEGAN
PREP TIME: 10 MINUTES / COOK TIME: 15 MINUTES

This colorful vegetable skillet is faster to make and tastes just as good as any meat dish, in my opinion. Use these vegetables or the extra veggies you have on hand, like summer squash or corn.

2 tablespoons gluten-free soy sauce

2 tablespoons sesame oil, divided

1 tablespoon cornstarch

2 garlic cloves, minced

1 cup sugar snap peas

1 cup mushrooms, quartered

½ red bell pepper, sliced

14 ounces zucchini noodles (about 2 medium zucchini)

1. In a small bowl, combine the soy sauce, 1 table-spoon of sesame oil, and cornstarch. Set aside.

2. Heat the remaining oil in a medium skillet over medium heat. Add the garlic and cook for 2 to 3 minutes. Stir in the snap peas, mushroom, and bell pepper, and cook for 3 minutes, until vegetables are crisp-tender.

3. Add the sauce and cook, stirring occasionally, for 3 to 5 minutes more, until the sauce thickens. Stir in the zucchini noodles and continue to cook for 2 minutes. Remove from the heat and serve.

ADD IT: For a boost of extra protein, add 1 cup of frozen unshelled edamame toward the end of the cooking time in step 2.

Per Serving: Calories: 210; Total fat: 14g; Total carbs: 18g; Protein: 6g; Fiber: 4g; Sugar: 7g; Sodium: 926mg

BURRITO ZUCCHINI BOATS

SUPER QUICK, VEGETARIAN
PREP TIME: 15 MINUTES / COOK TIME: 20 MINUTES

Burritos are usually way too much food for one serving—and yet I can eat an entire one in a flash. These Mexican favorites typically combine rice and a tortilla, which is a double-whammy if you're trying to be mindful of your carbohydrate intake. This zucchini boat is a healthy option if you don't want to give up that burrito taste.

1 large zucchini, halved lengthwise

Salt

Freshly ground black pepper

1 tablespoon extra-virgin olive oil

¼ cup canned black beans, drained and rinsed

1 small tomato, diced

½ small red onion, diced

1 jalapeño pepper, seeded and diced

1 teaspoon cumin

½ teaspoon chili powder

½ cup shredded Monterey Jack cheese

2 medium limes (1 to squeeze for juice, 1 quartered for garnish), divided

1 tablespoon chopped fresh cilantro, for garnish

1. Preheat the oven to 350°F.

2. Scoop out the insides of the zucchini and place the zucchini halves cut-side up in a casserole dish. Drizzle the insides with oil and season with salt and pepper. Bake for 10 minutes, or until zucchini turns bright green and begins to soften.

3. In a bowl, add the beans, tomato, onion, jalapeño pepper, cumin, chili powder, and a sprinkle of salt. Toss to combine, and divide the mixture between the 2 zucchini boats. Sprinkle each zucchini with half the Monterey Jack cheese. Bake for 15 to 20 minutes, or until the cheese is bubbly and golden brown.

4. Allow the boats to cool for 5 to 10 minutes, then squeeze the juice of 1 lime over both. Garnish each plate with the remaining lime wedges and cilantro, and serve.

ADD IT: Add ½ cup of corn kernels to the bean mixture for more color and extra flavor.

Per Serving: Calories: 243; Total fat: 17g; Total carbs: 15g; Protein: 12g; Fiber: 5g; Sugar: 5g; Sodium: 257mg

FRIED EGG AND PEPPER SANDWICH

SUPER QUICK, VEGETARIAN, COMFORT FOOD
PREP TIME: 10 MINUTES / COOK TIME: 15 MINUTES

This sandwich is one of my childhood favorites. For a deliciously salty and umami kick, I add olives to my fried egg sandwich instead of cheese. This sandwich proves you don't need complicated ingredients to have a tasty and indulgent dinner in minutes.

2 large eggs

7 tablespoons milk

1 tablespoon extra-virgin olive oil

1 medium bell pepper, cut into ½-inch-wide strips

½ onion, sliced

½ teaspoon red wine vinegar

Salt

Freshly ground black pepper

1 tablespoon unsalted butter

1 Italian bread loaf, cut lengthwise

⅓ cup pitted Kalamata olives

1 tablespoon fresh basil

1. In a small bowl, beat the eggs and milk with a whisk, and season with salt and pepper.

2. Heat the oil in a medium skillet over medium-high heat. Add the peppers, onion, and vinegar, and season with salt and pepper. Cook for 5 to 7 minutes, or until the peppers are tender. Set aside.

3. In the same skillet over medium heat, melt the butter. Pour in the egg mixture, and cook, stirring occasionally, until the eggs are set, 3 to 5 minutes.

4. Arrange the pepper and eggs on one side of the bread. Top with the olives and basil. Close the sandwich and cut in half.

Per Serving: Calories: 835; Total fat: 29g; Total carbs: 117g; Protein: 28g; Fiber: 8g; Sugar: 9g; Sodium: 1639mg

CRISPY TOFU SUMMER ROLLS

SUPER QUICK, VEGAN

PREP TIME: 20 MINUTES / COOK TIME: 10 MINUTES

skillet

serves
2

These rolls make for a deliciously healthy meal, loaded with flavor, crunch, and all the colors of the rainbow! I used my favorite veggies for this recipe, but feel free to substitute whatever crunchy vegetables you have on hand.

1 (14-ounce) block extra-firm tofu, drained, patted dry, and cubed

2 tablespoons cornstarch

Salt

2 tablespoons vegetable oil

1 tablespoon hoisin sauce

1 tablespoon freshly squeezed lime juice

1 teaspoon hot sauce, such as Sriracha

1 teaspoon finely chopped peanuts (optional)

4 (8-inch) rice paper sheets

8 butter lettuce leaves

½ cucumber, cut into matchsticks

½ carrot, cut into matchsticks

½ cup bean sprouts

1 tablespoon chopped fresh mint (optional)

1. In a bowl, combine the tofu with the cornstarch and season with salt. Mix gently to coat evenly.

2. Heat the oil in a skillet over medium-high heat. Add the tofu and fry, stirring often, until the cubes are evenly golden brown and crispy on all sides, about 10 minutes. Set aside.

3. In a small bowl, combine the hoisin sauce, lime juice, and hot sauce. Sprinkle with peanuts (if using), and set aside.

4. Pour very hot water in a shallow dish or pie plate to a depth of ½ inch. Soak the rice paper sheets, 1 at a time, in the hot water until softened, about 30 seconds. Arrange the sheets on a clean, flat work surface.

5. Place 2 butter lettuce leaves on each rice paper sheet. Arrange the tofu, cucumber, carrot, bean sprouts, and mint leaves (if using), on the tops of the rice paper sheets. Fold the opposite sides of each sheet over the filling, and roll up. Serve with the hoisin sauce mixture.

PREP HACK: Dry tofu thoroughly with a clean kitchen towel or paper towels before frying to prevent the oil from spattering.

Per Serving: Calories: 437; Total fat: 25g; Total carbs: 23g; Protein: 28g; Fiber: 2g; Sugar: 5g; Sodium: 505mg

TOFU THAI GREEN CURRY

SUPER QUICK, COMFORT FOOD, GLUTEN-FREE, VEGAN
PREP TIME: 10 MINUTES / COOK TIME: 15 MINUTES

Curry in 30 minutes—what a dream! This recipe's secret is freshening up store-bought curry paste by frying it. This essential step makes a really great green curry.

1 tablespoon extra-virgin olive oil

2 tablespoons green curry paste

3 cups vegetable stock

1 can coconut milk

3 Thai lime leaves

1 (14-ounce) block firm tofu, drained, patted dry, and cubed

1 cup white mushrooms, quartered

14 ounces zucchini noodles (about 2 medium zucchini)

Salt

Thai basil leaves, for garnish (optional)

4 lime wedges, for garnish (optional)

1. Heat the oil in a Dutch oven over medium-high heat. Add the curry paste and cook, stirring occasionally, for 2 to 3 minutes.

2. Mix in the stock, coconut milk, and lime leaves, and bring to a simmer.

3. Add the tofu and mushroom, reduce the heat to medium-low, and cook for 5 minutes.

4. Add the zucchini noodles and season with salt. Cook for 1 minute.

5. Divide the curry into 2 bowls and garnish with basil leaves (if using), and lime wedges (if using). And serve.

ADD IT: For a little more green, add a cup of frozen green peas or edamame with the tofu and mushrooms.

Per Serving: Calories: 865; Total fat: 76g; Total carbs: 35g; Protein: g; Fiber: 11g; Sugar: 18g; Sodium: 969mg

GRILLED EGGPLANT SANDWICH

SUPER QUICK, VEGETARIAN
PREP TIME: 15 MINUTES / COOK TIME: 15 MINUTES

sheet pan

serves
2

I have found myself enjoying eggplant more and more. When cooked right, it's lusciously tender with crispy edges. Grilling the eggplant and putting it in a sandwich with a caprese topping is an excellent way to get everyone to enjoy this vegetable.

1 small eggplant, cut lengthwise into ¼-inch-thick slices

2 tablespoons extra-virgin olive oil, divided

Salt

Freshly ground black pepper

¾ cup (about 3 ounces) fresh mozzarella, thinly sliced

2 (6-inch) French sandwich rolls, sliced in half lengthwise

1 garlic clove, finely minced

1 medium tomato, cut into ½-inch slices

4 large fresh basil leaves, torn

1. Preheat the broiler. Brush the eggplant slices on both sides with 1 tablespoon of olive oil, season with salt and pepper, and place them on a baking sheet. Broil for 10 minutes, or until tender. Place the mozzarella on top of the eggplant slices and return to oven for 1 minute. Remove and set aside..

2. Place the French rolls on the baking sheet and brush with 1 tablespoon of oil. Sprinkle with garlic, and broil for 3 minutes, or until the rolls are crisp on the outside.

3. Layer the eggplant and tomatoes in the French rolls, top with basil, and sandwich with the top half of the bread to serve.

USE IT AGAIN: Use any leftover basil in another recipe, such as Fried Egg and Pepper Sandwich (see page 60) or Bruschetta Grilled Chicken (see page 99).

Per Serving: Calories: 508; Total fat: 25g; Total carbs: 55g; Protein: 18g; Fiber: 10g; Sugar: 10g; Sodium: 732mg

EGGPLANT PARMESAN

VEGETARIAN
PREP TIME: 15 MINUTES / COOK TIME: 4 HOURS

This slow cooker eggplant parmesan is perfect for entertaining, so if you're having company over, just double the ingredient amounts. Everyone will think you spent all day in the kitchen. In reality, making this cheesy delight requires minimal effort.

1 large eggplant, cut into ½-inch-thick rounds

Salt

2 large eggs

⅓ cup bread crumbs

½ cup grated Parmesan cheese

1 teaspoon Italian seasoning

1 cup marinara sauce, divided

½ cup mozzarella cheese, sliced

1 tablespoon fresh basil, plus more for garnish

1. Place the eggplant slices on paper towels. Sprinkle with salt and let them sit for 20 minutes. Rinse the slices, then blot dry.

2. Whisk the eggs in a small bowl.

3. In a separate medium bowl, combine the bread crumbs, Parmesan cheese, and Italian seasoning.

4. Spread ⅓ cup of marinara sauce on the bottom of the slow cooker. Dip each slice of eggplant in the egg, then dredge in the bread crumb mixture. Lay the slices in an even layer in the slow cooker. Add ⅓ cup of marinara sauce, ¼ cup of the mozzarella cheese, and the basil. Repeat the layers, ending with the mozzarella cheese. Cover and cook on low for 4 hours. Garnish with more basil, and serve.

COOKING TIP: This can also be made in the oven. Follow all the steps as directed, but place in a casserole dish. Bake at 425°F for 20 to 25 minutes, or until the eggplant is tender and browned. Garnish with basil.

Per Serving: Calories: 370; Total fat: 17g; Total carbs: 33g; Protein: 24g; Fiber: 10g; Sugar: 11g; Sodium: 689mg

MUSHROOM AND BLACK BEAN TORTILLA CASSEROLE

COMFORT FOOD, VEGETARIAN
PREP TIME: 15 MINUTES / COOK TIME: 25 MINUTES

Who doesn't love a hearty casserole in the winter? This Mexican-inspired casserole is full of good-for-you ingredients, and it tastes even better the next day, which is why I've planned for this recipe to create some leftovers. Remove the gluten from this dish by using gluten-free corn tortillas.

2 ripe avocados, peeled and pitted

1 tablespoon freshly squeezed lime juice

Salt

6 small (6-inch) corn tortillas, warmed and halved (total of 12)

1 cup cremini or button mushrooms, trimmed and quartered

1 cup canned black beans, drained and rinsed

¾ cup frozen corn kernels, thawed

½ cup tomato salsa

1 cup shredded Mexican four-cheese blend

1 poblano chile, halved, seeded, and cut into ½-inch slices (optional)

1. Preheat the oven to 400°F.

2. In a small bowl, make a quick guacamole by mashing the avocado with the lime juice, and season with salt. Set aside.

3. In a casserole dish, arrange 4 tortilla halves in the bottom. Top with half each of the mushrooms, beans, corn, and salsa. Sprinkle with ⅓ cup of the cheese and a pinch of salt. Repeat the layering process once more, then top with the remaining 4 tortilla halves. Sprinkle the top with the remaining ¾ cup of cheese.

4. Cover with foil and bake until the center is hot and the cheese melts, about 15 to 20 minutes. Uncover, then bake until cheese is bubbling, about 5 minutes more. Serve with guacamole, and poblano chiles (if using).

ADD IT: Add 1 cup of diced sweet potatoes to the layers for an even heartier meal.

Per Serving: Calories: 851; Total fat: 48g; Total carbs: 85g; Protein: 33g; Fiber: 26g; Sugar: 4g; Sodium: 583mg

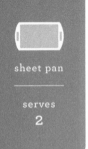
BROCCOLI AND SWEET POTATO SHEET PAN DINNER

GLUTEN-FREE, VEGAN

PREP TIME: 15 MINUTES / COOK TIME: 35 MINUTES

After a long day at work, you want something easy to assemble and a snap to clean up. This delectable sheet pan dinner fits the bill. It also makes for a well-balanced meal, providing a healthy source of protein (tofu) as well as good fats (olive oil), carbs (sweet potato), and green vegetables (broccoli).

1 small sweet potato, cut into 1-inch cubes (about 2 cups)

3 tablespoons extra-virgin olive oil, divided

1 (14-ounce) block firm tofu, cut into 1½-inch cubes

1 cup broccoli florets

2 garlic cloves, finely chopped

2 jalapeño peppers, seeded and sliced

1 teaspoon dried rosemary, crushed

½ teaspoon paprika

Salt

Freshly ground black pepper

1. Preheat the oven to 400°F.

2. Place the sweet potatoes on a baking sheet. Add 1 tablespoon of the oil and toss to evenly coat. Spread the potatoes in an even layer and roast for 15 minutes. Remove the pan from the oven.

3. Add the tofu, broccoli, garlic, and jalapeño peppers to the pan around the sweet potatoes. Sprinkle with the remaining 2 tablespoons of olive oil, rosemary, and paprika. Season with salt and pepper. Return to the oven for 15 to 20 minutes, until the broccoli is tender, tossing once halfway through. Serve immediately.

Per Serving: Calories: 374; Total fat: 30g; Total carbs: 15g; Protein: 19g; Fiber: 5g; Sugar: 5g; Sodium: 128mg

VEGETARIAN CHILI

GLUTEN-FREE, VEGETARIAN

PREP TIME: 15 MINUTES / COOK TIME: 20 MINUTES

electric
pressure
cooker

serves
2

This vegetarian chili is naturally gluten free and packed with plant-based protein. The electric pressure cooker saves time, and because it eliminates the need to sauté the veggies in oil, it reduces total fat and calories. To make this chili vegan, simply serve it without the cheese.

½ onion, diced

½ bell pepper, diced

1 carrot, peeled and diced

1 cup canned pinto beans, drained and rinsed

1 cup canned black beans, drained and rinsed

1 tablespoon tomato paste

3 cups vegetable stock

1 tablespoon cumin

2 garlic cloves, minced

Salt

Shredded cheddar cheese, for garnish

Fresh cilantro, for garnish

1. In an electric pressure cooker, add the onion, bell pepper, carrot, pinto beans, black beans, tomato paste, stock, cumin, and garlic. Stir well.

2. Close the lid and cook at high pressure for 10 minutes. Let the pressure release naturally, about 10 minutes. Quick release the remaining pressure in the pot (if any), and open the lid.

3. Stir the chili and season with salt. Serve warm topped with shredded cheddar cheese and cilantro.

COOKING TIP: To make this in a pot or Dutch oven, heat the oil, then add the onion and garlic, and cook for 3 to 5 minutes. Add the bell pepper and carrot, and cook for 5 to 8 minutes. Add the beans, tomato paste, stock, and cumin. Cook for 20 minutes on low. Season with salt and top with shredded cheddar and cilantro.

Per Serving: Calories: 434; Total fat: 11g; Total carbs: 61g; Protein: 26g; Fiber: 19g; Sugar: 10g; Sodium: 499mg

ONE-POT VEGETABLE JAMBALAYA

GLUTEN-FREE, VEGETARIAN
PREP TIME: 15 MINUTES / COOK TIME: 30 MINUTES

Like the many soups and stews that see us through winter, jambalaya accommodates whatever ingredients you have on hand. Jambalaya has more fiery freshness than most cold-weather staples, and this version is quick and easy to make. With Creole flavors, rice, and a can of tomatoes, you'll have dinner done in less time than it takes to put together a Louis Armstrong playlist.

1 tablespoon
    unsalted butter

½ small onion, diced

½ bell pepper, chopped

1 celery stalk, chopped

1 cup canned diced
    tomatoes

Red pepper flakes
    (optional)

Salt

Freshly ground
    black pepper

2 cups vegetable stock

1 cup long-grain white rice

2 tablespoons Creole
    seasoning (see "Swap
    It" tip)

1. In a Dutch oven over medium-high heat, melt the butter. Add the onion, bell pepper, and celery, and cook, stirring occasionally, for 5 minutes or until the vegetables are soft.

2. Stir in the tomatoes and red pepper flakes (if using), and season with salt and pepper.

3. Add the stock, rice, and Creole seasoning, stir to combine, and bring to a boil. Reduce the heat to medium-low, cover, and simmer for 20 minutes, or until the rice is tender, giving it a stir around the halfway point. Serve warm.

SWAP IT: If you can't find Creole seasoning, make your own! Mix together equal amounts of paprika, garlic powder, salt, black pepper, cayenne, onion powder, dried oregano, and dried thyme.

Per Serving: Calories: 443; Total fat: 7g; Total carbs: 86g; Protein: 9g; Fiber: 4g; Sugar: 8g; Sodium: 2519mg

VEGETARIAN QUINOA BIBIMBAP

pot

serves
2

GLUTEN-FREE, VEGAN
PREP TIME: 15 MINUTES / COOK TIME: 25 MINUTES

I love vegetables, but some days I just don't want another salad for dinner. This flavorful Korean-inspired dish is a great way to get your veggies and make them interesting. The term "bibimbap," literally "mixed rice," has come to mean a mixing together of various ingredients. I use quinoa rather than rice for a lower-calorie and -carb version, but feel free to use rice if you'd prefer.

FOR THE SAUCE

1 tablespoon gluten-free
  soy sauce

1 tablespoon hot sauce,
  such as Sriracha

2 teaspoons sugar

1 teaspoon sesame seeds

1 teaspoon sesame oil

1 teaspoon minced garlic

FOR THE BIBIMBAP

1 carrot, cut into
  matchsticks

2 cups baby spinach

1 cup sliced shiitake
  mushrooms

2 cups water

1 cup quinoa

Salt

1 small cucumber, julienned

1 scallion, thinly sliced,
  for garnish

Toasted sesame seeds, for
  garnish (optional)

½ cup Napa cabbage
  kimchi, for garnish
  (optional)

1. To make the sauce, in a small bowl, mix together the soy sauce, hot sauce, sugar, sesame seeds, sesame oil, and garlic. Set aside.

2. To make the bibimbap, boil a pot of water, and add the carrots. Simmer for 2 to 4 minutes until crisp-tender. Remove the carrots from the pot using a slotted spoon. Set aside.

3. Add the spinach to the pot of water, and boil, 1 to 2 minutes, until the spinach is wilted. Remove the spinach from the pot using a slotted spoon, and set aside to cool. Once the spinach has cooled, squeeze well to remove excess water, then slice thinly.

4. Add the mushrooms to the pot, and boil for 2 to 3 minutes. Remove the mushrooms from the pot using a slotted spoon. When the mushrooms are cool enough to handle, squeeze them to remove excess water, then slice thinly.

VEGETARIAN QUINOA BIBIMBAP Continues

5. In the same pot, bring 2 cups of water to a boil over medium-high heat. Add the quinoa, then reduce the heat to a simmer. Cover, and cook until the quinoa is fluffy and has absorbed all the water, 10 to 15 minutes. Uncover, and fluff the quinoa with a fork. Salt to taste and stir to combine.

6. Divide the quinoa between 2 bowls. Top each bowl with carrots, spinach, mushrooms, and cucumbers. Drizzle each bowl with the sauce. Garnish with scallions, toasted sesame seeds (if using), and kimchi (if using), and serve.

Per Serving: Calories: 447; Total fat: 9g; Total carbs: 80g; Protein: 16g; Fiber: 10g; Sugar: 11g; Sodium: 947mg

SHEET PAN RATATOUILLE GNOCCHI

VEGAN
PREP TIME: 15 MINUTES / COOK TIME: 25 MINUTES

One of my go-to recipes for dinner, ratatouille is a classic dish from the south of France that showcases fresh summer produce. My sheet pan version includes gnocchi to make it a meal-in-one. This low-maintenance dinner can be served hot or at room temperature. If your eggplant is larger than your zucchini, you can feel free to cut the slices into half-moons so they're the same size as the zucchini. Cutting your veggies into roughly the same size will help them roast more evenly in the oven.

1 garlic clove, minced

⅓ cup extra-virgin olive oil

1 teaspoon dried thyme

Salt

1 cup potato gnocchi, fresh or shelf-stable

1 small eggplant, cut into ½-inch slices

1 zucchini, cut into ½-inch slices

2 tomatoes, quartered

1 yellow bell pepper, cut into ½-inch spears

Red pepper flakes (optional)

1. Preheat the oven to 400°F.

2. In a large bowl, combine the garlic, oil, and thyme, and season with salt. Add the gnocchi and chopped vegetables, and toss to coat.

3. Spread the mixture in an even layer on a baking sheet. Roast until the squash is tender but not mushy, about 25 minutes, stirring at the half-way mark.

4. Divide the ratatouille between 2 plates and sprinkle with red pepper flakes (if using), and serve.

USE IT AGAIN: Have extra gnocchi on hand? Use them in Sun-Dried Tomato Tortellini Soup (see page 40) instead of the tortellini.

Per Serving: Calories: 543; Total fat: 35g; Total carbs: 54g; Protein: 11g; Fiber: 12g; Sugar: 15g; Sodium: 272mg

GARLIC-PARMESAN PASTA

SUPER QUICK, 5-INGREDIENT, VEGETARIAN
PREP TIME: 10 MINUTES / COOK TIME: 10 MINUTES

It's easy to love this dish, which features hot buttered pasta tossed in a creamy, garlicky, Parmesan sauce. Simple, yet elegant and so delicious, it is great for date night or even a weeknight dinner because it is ready in under 30 minutes—yay!

Salt

4 ounces fresh or dried pasta

2 tablespoons unsalted butter

2 garlic cloves, minced

1 tablespoon freshly grated Parmesan cheese

2 tablespoons chopped fresh parsley

Freshly ground black pepper

Red pepper flakes, for garnish (optional)

1. Bring a medium pot of salted water to a boil. Add the pasta and cook until al dente, about 4 minutes for fresh pasta, and 8 to 10 minutes for dried. Reserve ½ cup of the pasta water in a small bowl, and set aside.

2. In the same pot, melt the butter over medium heat. Add the garlic and cook, stirring frequently, until fragrant, 1 to 2 minutes. Remove from the heat.

3. Add the pasta to the garlic mixture. Add a little of the reserved pasta water, if needed to coat all the pasta. Stir in the Parmesan cheese and parsley, and season with salt and pepper.

4. Divide between 2 plates and garnish with red pepper flakes (if using), and serve.

Per Serving: Calories: 280; Total fat: 14g; Total carbs: 32g; Protein: 8g; Fiber: 0g; Sugar: 0g; Sodium: 209mg

Seafood

HONEY-GARLIC GLAZED SHRIMP LETTUCE WRAPS

SUPER QUICK, GLUTEN-FREE
PREP TIME: 15 MINUTES / COOK TIME: 10 MINUTES

Raise your hand if you are a big fan of Chinese food. If so, I have just the recipe for you. You can make this at home in about 20 minutes—faster than delivery! And this tasty, sweet, honey-infused meal is just as good, if not better, than what you'd pick up at your local Chinese takeout.

2 tablespoons honey

1 tablespoon gluten-free soy sauce

2 tablespoons extra-virgin olive oil

1 garlic clove, minced

½ pound asparagus, trimmed and cut into 1-inch pieces

½ pound shrimp, peeled and deveined

6 to 8 butter lettuce leaves

¼ cup fresh cilantro leaves or cilantro microgreens, for garnish

1 scallion, thinly sliced, for garnish

1 teaspoon sesame seeds, for garnish (optional)

1. In a small bowl, combine the honey and soy sauce. Set aside.

2. Heat the oil in a skillet over medium-high heat. Add the garlic and cook for 2 minutes. Add the asparagus and cook, stirring frequently, until tender, 2 to 3 minutes. Add the shrimp and cook for 2 to 3 minutes, until pink. Stir in the honey mixture and cook, stirring, until well combined and slightly thickened, 1 to 2 minutes.

3. Serve the shrimp and asparagus in the lettuce leaves or "cups," topped with cilantro, scallions, and sesame seeds (if using).

SWAP IT: Try salmon instead of shrimp. Just season 2 (6-ounce) salmon fillets with salt and pepper. Over medium-high heat, sear the salmon for 3 to 4 minutes on each side, until browned. Flake the salmon in large chunks with a fork and add back to the skillet with the honey mixture to cook together.

Per Serving: Calories: 316; Total fat: 15g; Total carbs: 24g; Protein: 26g; Fiber: 3g; Sugar: 20g; Sodium: 586mg

HONEY-MUSTARD SALMON PASTRIES WITH ASPARAGUS

sheet pan

serves
2

COMFORT FOOD

PREP TIME: 20 MINUTES / COOK TIME: 25 MINUTES

This ideal fuss-free, pain-free, stove-free recipe is perfect for lazy days when you want something easy to make, but still decadent, for dinner. These flaky salmon parcels feature regularly in our household. They are elegant enough for company too, if you have guests you want to impress.

1 tablespoon Dijon mustard

½ tablespoon honey

2 tablespoons extra-virgin olive oil, divided

1 frozen puff pastry sheet, thawed, but still cold

Flour, for dusting

2 (6-ounce) salmon fillets

1 egg, lightly beaten

1 bunch thin asparagus spears, trimmed

1 tablespoon grated Parmesan cheese (optional)

Salt

1½ teaspoons freshly squeezed lemon juice

1. Preheat the oven to 400°F.

2. In a small bowl, mix the mustard, honey, and 1 tablespoon of olive oil. Set aside.

3. Unfold the puff pastry onto a lightly floured work surface. Cut each sheet in half. Place one salmon fillet on each puff pastry rectangle, and spread the Dijon sauce on top of each piece. Brush the egg wash around the edges of each sheet, and fold over the sides to cover the salmon. Brush the tops with the egg wash, and place the pastries folded-side down, on one side of a baking sheet.

HONEY-MUSTARD SALMON PASTRIES WITH ASPARAGUS Continues

4. Add the asparagus in a single layer on the other side of the baking sheet. Drizzle with the remaining 1 tablespoon of olive oil and toss to coat. Sprinkle with Parmesan cheese (if using), and season with salt.

5. Bake for 20 minutes, or until the pastry is golden and puffed. Drizzle the lemon juice over the pastries before serving.

ADD IT: Add a little green to the pastries with some frozen spinach, thawed and drained. Strain all the excess water with a mesh sieve or strainer, and squeeze out any remaining water. Top each salmon fillet with a spoonful of spinach in the puff pastries. Proceed as directed.

Per Serving: Calories: 1142; Total fat: 76g; Total carbs: 59g; Protein: 53g; Fiber: 4g; Sugar: 7g; Sodium: 571mg

MUSSELS IN LEMONGRASS BROTH

SUPER QUICK, GLUTEN-FREE
PREP TIME: 10 MINUTES / COOK TIME: 10 MINUTES

If you are looking for a decadent broth for date night or as a dinner-party starter, break out this amazing dish, which pairs the earthy undertones of lemongrass with the seafood punch of mussels. The broth melds the flavors of sweet coconut milk, fresh lemongrass, and pungent lime juice. What could be better? As you clean the mussels, make sure their shells are tightly closed. Discard any opened or cracked mussels.

2 ounces rice noodles

2 cups fish stock

1 tablespoon shredded ginger

1 lemongrass stalk, finely chopped

1 cup coconut milk

2 pounds mussels, washed thoroughly

Salt

1 tablespoon tightly packed cilantro, for garnish

4 lime wedges, for garnish

1. In a pot, bring water to a boil. Add the rice noodles and cook until al dente, 3 to 5 minutes. Rinse the noodles under cold water, and set aside.

2. In the pot, bring the stock, ginger, and lemongrass to a boil. Add the coconut milk and mussels, and cook for 3 minutes, or until they have opened. Discard any mussels that do not open. Season the broth with salt.

3. Divide the noodles between 2 bowls and top with the soup and mussels. Garnish with cilantro and lime wedges, and serve.

SWAP IT: Use scallops instead of mussels, if preferred. Cook as directed, but when adding the coconut milk, add 14 ounces of bay scallops, and cook for 5 minutes. Continue as directed.

Per Serving: Calories: 534; Total fat: 35g; Total carbs: 35g; Protein: 23g; Fiber: 3g; Sugar: 4g; Sodium: 928mg

SHRIMP 'N' GRITS

GLUTEN-FREE
PREP TIME: 15 MINUTES / COOK TIME: 3 OR 7 HOURS,
DEPENDING ON COOKING METHOD

The lightness of the shrimp, paired with the satiating creaminess of the grits, makes this dish a simple and scrumptious meal that will have your friends and family asking for more. You don't need to constantly watch and stir the grits with this slow cooker recipe. You can set it and forget it until it's time to add the shrimp at the end.

1 cup stone-ground grits

½ cup shredded
cheddar cheese

½ cup grated
Parmesan cheese

3¼ cups chicken stock

½ tablespoon
garlic powder

½ tablespoon
onion powder

Salt

½ pound large shrimp,
peeled and deveined

Freshly ground
black pepper

Chopped scallions,
for garnish

1. In a slow cooker, combine the grits, cheddar cheese, Parmesan cheese, stock, garlic powder, onion powder, and salt. Stir to combine. Cook on high for 3 hours, or low for 7 hours, until the grits are soft and cooked through.

2. Add the shrimp to the slow cooker. Cover and cook for another 5 to 8 minutes, until the shrimp are pink. Ladle into 2 bowls, arranging the shrimp on top of the grits. Season with black pepper and garnish with scallions before serving.

Per Serving: Calories: 390; Total fat: 16g; Total carbs: 20g; Protein: 43g; Fiber: 1g; Sugar: 1g; Sodium: 794mg

ZUPPA DE PESCE

SUPER QUICK, GLUTEN-FREE
PREP TIME: 15 MINUTES / COOK TIME: 15 MINUTES

Simple and wholesome, this comforting meal reminds me of home. Get into your pajamas, put on your favorite show, and enjoy a bowl of this sea-food stew—it's a great way to spend an evening.

2 cups water

1 cup seafood stock

1 tablespoon Old Bay seasoning

Salt

1 medium red potato, quartered

1 ear corn, cut into 4 pieces

1 pound jumbo shrimp, tail on and deveined

4 ounces sea scallops

½ teaspoon red pepper (optional)

1 tablespoon chopped fresh parsley (optional)

1. In a Dutch oven, bring the water, stock, Old Bay, and salt, to taste, to a boil.

2. Stir in the potato and corn, and cook for 8 to 10 minutes, or until the potato is tender.

3. Add the shrimp and scallops and cook for 3 to 4 minutes, until cooked through.

4. Sprinkle with red pepper and fresh parsley (if using) before serving.

ADD IT: Include any sturdy fish or shellfish you wish in this stew, such as mussels, clams, or cod.

Per Serving: Calories: 441; Total fat: 6g; Total carbs: 33g; Protein: 60g; Fiber: 4g; Sugar: 3g; Sodium: 1664mg

CRABMEAT FETTUCCINE

SUPER QUICK
PREP TIME: 10 MINUTES / COOK TIME: 10 MINUTES

This quick and easy pasta recipe uses crabmeat, which can be canned or fresh. You don't have to add many ingredients to make this dish super tasty—mustard, dill, and capers pack giant flavors in small quantities. This recipe can be easily doubled or tripled, making it a great choice for occasions when you have the whole family over.

Salt

4 ounces fresh or dried fettuccine or linguine

2 tablespoons extra-virgin olive oil

1 tablespoon freshly squeezed lemon juice

1 tablespoon chopped fresh dill

½ tablespoon whole-grain mustard

½ tablespoon red pepper flakes (optional)

8 ounces crabmeat (fresh or canned)

1 teaspoon capers, rinsed

Freshly ground black pepper

1. Bring a pot of salted water to a boil. Add the pasta and simmer until al dente, 4 to 5 minutes if using fresh, or 8 to 12 minutes if using dried. Drain the pasta, and reserve ½ cup of pasta water. Set aside.

2. In a small bowl, combine the oil, lemon juice, dill, mustard, red pepper flakes (if using), and a pinch of salt. Stir until well mixed, adding a little of the reserved pasta water, if needed, to thin the sauce.

3. Divide the pasta between 2 plates. Add the crabmeat, capers, and mustard-dill sauce, and toss to coat. Season with black pepper and serve immediately.

SWAP IT: Try this with smoked salmon. Cook the pasta, then divide between 2 plates. Combine 3 or 4 slices of smoked salmon with the capers and mustard-dill mixture. Divide the salmon over the pasta. Toss, and season with black pepper.

Per Serving: Calories: 378; Total fat: 17g; Total carbs: 33g; Protein: 10g; Fiber: 1g; Sugar: 0g; Sodium: 761mg

LEMON AND PARSLEY FRIED FISH

SUPER QUICK, GLUTEN-FREE
PREP TIME: 10 MINUTES / COOK TIME: 10 MINUTES

Fried to perfection, this flaky white fish is mouthwateringly soft on the inside and crunchy on the outside. Lemon and parsley and a side of spinach finish it off perfectly.

¼ cup chopped fresh flat-leaf parsley

1 tablespoon lemon zest, plus 4 lemon wedges for squeezing and serving

Salt

Freshly ground black pepper

2 tablespoons vegetable oil

2 (6-ounce) fillets white fish (such as tilapia, halibut, or cod)

1 tablespoon extra-virgin olive oil

1 shallot, thinly sliced

4 cups fresh spinach

1. In a bowl, combine the parsley and lemon zest, and season with salt and pepper. Press the lemon and parsley mixture onto both sides of the fish.

2. Heat the vegetable oil in a skillet over high heat. Place the fish in the pan and cook for 1 to 2 minutes on each side, or until the fish is cooked through and flakes with a fork. Remove the pan from the heat, and squeeze the juice of 1 lemon wedge over the fish.

3. Wipe out the skillet with a paper towel, and heat the olive oil over medium-high heat. Add the shallot and cook 2 to 3 minutes, until soft. Add the spinach, season with salt and pepper, and cook 3 to 4 minutes, until the spinach is wilted. Serve the fish with the spinach and lemon wedges on the side.

Per Serving: Calories: 344; Total fat: 23g; Total carbs: 4g; Protein: 34g; Fiber: 2g; Sugar: 0g; Sodium: 190mg

THAI ZOODLE FISH CURRY

SUPER QUICK, GLUTEN-FREE
PREP TIME: 15 MINUTES / COOK TIME: 10 MINUTES

Fish curry is a great option when you're looking for a spicy meal that's still light, and this one tastes just like something you'd get at a restaurant—but you can enjoy it in the comfort of your own home!

2 cups vegetable stock

1 cup coconut milk

1 tablespoon red
curry paste

1 tablespoon gluten-free
soy sauce

Salt

2 (6-ounce) cod fillets (or
other white fish)

2 medium zucchini,
spiralized

Fresh basil, for garnish

1 jalapeño pepper, sliced
(optional)

4 lime wedges, for
squeezing

1. In an electric pressure cooker, add the stock, coconut milk, curry paste, and soy sauce. Mix well and season with salt. Place the cod in the bottom of the pressure cooker.

2. Cover, and cook for 5 minutes on low pressure. When done, quick release the pressure.

3. Divide the zoodles between two bowls. Add the warm soup to the bowls and top with basil and jalapeño pepper (if using). Squeeze in lime juice, to taste, before serving.

COOKING TIP: To cook this on the stovetop, heat 1 tablespoon of olive oil in a pot over medium heat. Add the curry paste and cook, stirring, for 1 minute. Slowly add the stock to the pot and stir continually for 1 minute more. Add the fish and soy sauce; reduce heat to low and simmer for 15 minutes. Stir in the coconut milk and salt, to taste. Cook for about 3 minutes. Serve over the zoodles as instructed.

Per Serving: Calories: 497; Total fat: 33g; Total carbs: 19g; Protein: 37g; Fiber: 6g; Sugar: 11g; Sodium: 1201mg

GARLIC-LIME FISH TACOS

SUPER QUICK, GLUTEN-FREE
PREP TIME: 15 MINUTES / COOK TIME: 15 MINUTES

These tacos will quickly become a weeknight staple if you are a fan of fish. They come together quickly, and you can get creative with garnishes and salsas. This pairing of mild fish with creamy fresh avocado and lime juice, spicy jalapeño peppers and crunchy cabbage cannot be beat.

2 tablespoons extra-virgin olive oil, divided

½ small onion, chopped

2 garlic cloves, minced

Salt

½ pound lean white fish fillets (such as cod, halibut, or tilapia)

Freshly ground black pepper

6 small (6-inch) corn tortillas

1 cup shredded cabbage

1 medium avocado, sliced

2 teaspoons fresh cilantro, chopped

2 jalapeño peppers, sliced (optional)

2 tablespoons freshly squeezed lime juice

1. Heat 1 tablespoon of olive oil in a skillet over medium heat. Add the onion and sauté for 4 to 5 minutes. Add the garlic and cook, stirring frequently, for 2 minutes. Sprinkle with salt. Mix well, and set aside in a medium bowl.

2. Add the remaining 1 tablespoon of oil to the skillet over medium heat. Add the fish and cook, flipping once or twice, until the flesh starts to flake, about 5 minutes. Season with salt and pepper, and set aside. With a fork, break the fish into large pieces, and add to the bowl with the onion and garlic mixture, stirring to combine.

3. Heat a tortilla on the skillet or directly over the flame of a burner for 30 seconds to 1 minute on each side, or until warm and slightly browned.

4. To serve, add some cabbage on a warm tortilla. Top with the fish, avocado, cilantro, and jala-peño peppers (if using), lime juice, and salt and pepper to taste.

> **ADD IT:** When summer fruits are in season, con-sider adding 1 cup of chopped mango or peaches to your tacos.

Per Serving: Calories: 546; Total fat: 31g; Total carbs: 48g; Protein: 28g; Fiber: 12g; Sugar: 4g; Sodium: 166mg

MISO SALMON

SUPER QUICK, 5-INGREDIENT, GLUTEN-FREE
PREP TIME: 5 MINUTES / COOK TIME: 15 MINUTES

This salmon dish, in which the miso packs a rich umami punch, is a solid dinner option for busy nights. It's healthy and can be made quickly and conveniently in an electric pressure cooker. You will need a steamer rack or insert to make this dish.

2 cups mixed salad greens

2 tablespoons extra-virgin olive oil, divided

1 tablespoon balsamic vinegar

2 (6-ounce) salmon fillets

Salt

Freshly ground black pepper

2 tablespoons unsalted butter

1½ cups water

1 tablespoon freshly squeezed lemon juice

½ teaspoon white miso paste

1. In a medium bowl, mix the salad greens, 1 tablespoon of olive oil, and the balsamic vinegar. Divide the greens between 2 plates and set aside.

2. Season both sides of the salmon fillets with salt and pepper.

3. Turn the electric pressure cooker to the sauté or brown setting, and melt the butter. Place the salmon fillets inside. Brown both sides, about 3 minutes on each side, and set aside on a plate.

4. Add the water to the pressure cooker, and put a steamer rack inside. Place the seared salmon onto the steaming rack. Cover, and cook on low pressure for 2 minutes. When done, allow for 5 minutes of natural release, then quick release the remaining pressure (if any). Carefully transfer the salmon from the rack to 2 plates.

5. In a small bowl, combine the lemon juice, miso paste, and the remaining 1 tablespoon of olive oil. Drizzle over the salmon, and serve immediately.

COOKING TIP: To cook the salmon on the stove, season the fish and cook it in the melted butter in a skillet over medium-high heat for 4 minutes on each side, or until cooked through.

Per Serving: Calories: 640; Total fat: 47g; Total carbs: 4g; Protein: 41g; Fiber: 1g; Sugar: 0g; Sodium: 407mg

BROILED SWEET AND SPICY SALMON

SUPER QUICK, GLUTEN-FREE
PREP TIME: 15 MINUTES / COOK TIME: 15 MINUTES

Homemade sweet and spicy sauce tastes so much better than one that's bottled. This salmon dish is paired with a kicky cantaloupe salad. Serve it with rice for a fast and delicious dinner!

Nonstick cooking spray

2 tablespoons maple syrup

1 teaspoon
   cayenne pepper

2 (6-ounce) skinless
   salmon fillets

Salt

Freshly ground
   black pepper

¼ cantaloupe, peeled,
   seeded, and cut into
   1-inch slices

1 small English cucumber,
   halved and sliced

1 jalapeño pepper, halved
   lengthwise, seeded, and
   thinly sliced

2 small limes (for
   1 tablespoon lime
   juice and wedges, for
   squeezing), divided

1 tablespoon torn
   fresh mint

1. Heat the broiler with the oven rack in the top position.

2. Spray a rimmed baking sheet with cooking spray.

3. To make a glaze, in a small bowl, combine the maple syrup and cayenne pepper.

4. Arrange the salmon fillets on the prepared baking sheet. Season with salt and pepper, and brush the tops with half the glaze. Broil for 8 to 12 minutes, brushing with the remaining glaze halfway through. Set aside.

5. In a large bowl, combine the cantaloupe, cucumber, jalapeño pepper, lime juice, and mint, and season with salt. Mix well, and squeeze a lime wedge over the top to taste (if using). Serve the salad alongside the broiled fish. Enjoy!

Per Serving: Calories: 391; Total fat: 18g; Total carbs: 23g; Protein: 35g; Fiber: 2g; Sugar: 17g; Sodium: 183mg

TUNA RAVIOLI LASAGNA

COMFORT FOOD
PREP TIME: 10 MINUTES / COOK TIME: 40 MINUTES

If you're like me and have a hard time resisting the urge to stick your fork into a baked pasta dish as soon as it comes out of the oven, this recipe is for you. This twist on the comfort classic is rich and delicious—and easy to make.

FOR THE SAUCE

3 tablespoons
  unsalted butter

2 tablespoons
  all-purpose flour

1½ cups milk

1 tablespoon dry
  white wine

¼ cup Parmesan cheese

Salt

FOR THE LASAGNA

1 (9-ounce) package wild
  mushroom ravioli

1 cup whole-milk
  ricotta cheese

½ cup whole-milk
  mozzarella cheese

1 (5-ounce) can albacore
  tuna in oil, drained
  and flaked

½ cup frozen peas

½ cup bread crumbs

¼ cup grated
  Parmesan cheese

1 tablespoon chopped
  fresh parsley

1. Preheat the oven to 350°F.

2. To make the sauce, in a Dutch oven over medium heat, melt the butter. While the butter melts, add the flour and mix until the flour is fully blended into the butter. Slowly stir in the milk and wine. Sprinkle in the Parmesan cheese and salt, whisking until the mixture slightly thickened. Turn off the heat.

3. To make the lasagna, ladle two-thirds of the sauce from the pot into a bowl, leaving a layer of sauce on the bottom of the Dutch oven. Layer half of the ravioli, ricotta cheese, mozzarella cheese, and tuna in the Dutch oven and sprinkle with peas. Repeat this process for another layer, then top with the remaining sauce.

4. Cover with aluminum foil and bake for 25 minutes.

5. While the lasagna is baking, combine the bread crumbs, Parmesan cheese, and parsley in a medium bowl. When the lasagna is done, uncover the pot and sprinkle the top with the bread crumb mixture. Bake for 10 minutes more, or until the crumb mixture is golden brown, and serve.

PREP HACK: To make this freezer-friendly meal ahead of time, make the sauce then assemble the lasagna following steps 2 and 3, in a casserole dish. Wrap in plastic wrap, pressing down to remove the air. Cover with foil, label, and freeze for up to 2 months. Thaw in the fridge overnight and bake covered in a 375°F oven for 30 minutes, or until bubbly and pasta is cooked; then continue with step 5.

Per Serving: Calories: 1032; Total fat: 46g; Total carbs: 96g; Protein: 59g; Fiber: 5g; Sugar: 16g; Sodium: 1647mg

WASABI TUNA PASTA

SUPER QUICK
PREP TIME: 10 MINUTES / COOK TIME: 15 MINUTES

Sometimes simple food is the best food. This pasta dish wonderfully combines the umami flavors of wasabi and fresh parsley to deliver a mouthwatering meal with minimum fuss. Yes, please!

4 ounces fresh or dried angel hair pasta

1 cup frozen peas

2 tablespoons extra-virgin olive oil

1 tablespoon freshly squeezed lemon juice

½ tablespoon soy sauce

½ teaspoon wasabi paste

1 (5-ounce) can albacore tuna, in oil

1 teaspoon chopped fresh parsley

Freshly ground black pepper

1. Bring a pot of salted water to a boil and cook the pasta until al dente, about 2 minutes for fresh angel hair, or 5 to 6 minutes for dried. Add the peas to the pot in the last 2 minutes of cook time. Drain the pasta and peas. Set aside.

2. In a bowl, combine the olive oil, lemon juice, soy sauce, and wasabi paste.

3. Toss the pasta and peas with the tuna and wasabi mixture. To serve, top with the parsley and pepper, to taste.

SWAP IT: Instead of wasabi, you can try using horseradish for a kick.

Per Serving: Calories: 431; Total fat: 17g; Total carbs: 44g; Protein: 27g; Fiber: 5g; Sugar: 4g; Sodium: 367mg

6

Poultry

HONEY-GARLIC CHICKEN WINGS

COMFORT FOOD, GLUTEN-FREE
PREP TIME: 15 MINUTES, PLUS MARINATING TIME / COOK TIME: 20 MINUTES

Chicken wings are a must-have for warm summer nights. This recipe has the wings slathered in honey and soy sauce and cooked until tender and juicy—is your mouth watering yet?

¼ cup honey

2 tablespoons gluten-free soy sauce

1 teaspoon fresh ginger, grated

2 garlic cloves, minced

1 teaspoon chili powder (optional)

2 tablespoons sesame oil

1 pound chicken wings, cleaned, and halved

Sesame seeds, for garnish

1. In a bowl, mix together the honey, soy sauce, ginger, garlic, and chili powder (if using). Add the chicken wings. Marinate the chicken for a few hours or overnight in the fridge.

2. Heat an electric pressure cooker in sauté mode. Add the sesame oil to the pot, then add the wings, searing for 2 or 3 minutes on each side. The wings can be cooked in batches, if needed, to avoid crowding the pot.

3. Place the seared chicken wings in the pot, add the marinade, and cover and lock the lid. Cook on high pressure for 10 minutes.

4. Allow the pressure to release naturally, about 10 minutes, and remove the lid. Transfer the wings to a plate and garnish with sesame seeds, to serve.

> **PREP HACK:** Make this recipe ahead of time. The sauce and the wings will keep in an airtight container for up to four days in the fridge or four months in the freezer. To reheat, just thaw in the fridge overnight and bake for 20 minutes at 425°F.

Per Serving: Calories: 1003; Total fat: 63g; Total carbs: 62g; Protein: 47g; Fiber: 2g; Sugar: 35g; Sodium: 1642mg

HONEY-SESAME CHICKEN WITH MIXED BABY GREENS

SUPER QUICK, GLUTEN-FREE
PREP TIME: 10 MINUTES / COOK TIME: 15 MINUTES

This homemade sesame chicken recipe features crispy chicken pieces tossed in a sweet and savory honey sesame sauce and served on a bed of salad greens. The result is healthier than what you would get at a restaurant.

2 (4-ounce) skinless boneless chicken breasts, cut into bite-size pieces

Salt

Freshly ground black pepper

1 tablespoon vegetable or extra-virgin olive oil

2 garlic cloves, minced

¼ cup honey

2 tablespoons gluten-free soy sauce

2 tablespoons cornstarch

3 tablespoons cold water

1 tablespoon sesame seeds

2 cups spring mix baby lettuce

1 tablespoon red wine vinegar

⅓ cup chopped fresh cilantro

1. Season the chicken on both sides with salt and pepper.

2. Preheat the electric pressure cooker by selecting the sauté or brown function. Add the oil, garlic, and chicken to the pot. Sauté for 3 to 4 minutes, stirring to ensure the chicken is evenly cooked on all sides.

3. Stir in the honey and soy sauce. Cover, and cook on high pressure for 3 minutes. Quick release the pressure, and turn off the cooker.

4. In a small bowl, whisk together the cornstarch and cold water until smooth. Add it to the pot and use the brown or sauté function to simmer the sauce, stirring constantly, until it thickens, 5 to 7 minutes. Sprinkle with the sesame seeds.

5. In a medium bowl, toss the lettuce with the red wine vinegar and divide between 2 plates. Top each salad with the sesame chicken, then sprinkle with cilantro to serve.

Per Serving: Calories: 440; Total fat: 13g; Total carbs: 49g; Protein: 34g; Fiber: 2g; Sugar: 35g; Sodium: 1107mg

CHICKEN UDON SOUP WITH SOFT-COOKED EGG

PREP TIME: 10 MINUTES / COOK TIME: 30 MINUTES

This chicken udon soup feels like a fitting hello to winter and shorter days. It has a complex flavor—salty, sweet, earthy, fruity, and savory. I often find myself craving this protein-packed soup with oodles of noodles when the weather turns cold, especially if I'm fighting off a cold.

2 large eggs, cold

1 cup water

1 cup enoki mushrooms

2 (4-ounce) boneless
   skinless chicken breasts,
   cut into pieces

Salt

Freshly ground
   black pepper

1 teaspoon cornstarch

1 tablespoon sesame oil

2 garlic cloves, minced

4 cups chicken stock

1 tablespoon miso paste

2 cups (10-ounce) fresh
   udon noodles

1 scallion, sliced

1. In a medium pot, boil water. Remove from the heat. Add the cold eggs and 1 cup of cold water to the pot. Cover, and let sit for 15 minutes. Then remove the eggs with a ladle and transfer to a bowl of ice cold water to stop the cooking process. Discard the water in the pot and dry it with a towel.

2. While the eggs are cooling, cut the bottom 2 inches off the mushroom stems, and discard. Gently separate the mushroom strands.

3. In a medium bowl, season the chicken with salt and pepper, and add the cornstarch, tossing to coat.

4. In the same pot, heat the oil over medium-high heat. Add the chicken and garlic in one layer, and cook for 3 to 5 minutes on each side, moving the garlic on top of the chicken so the tender cloves don't burn. Continue cooking for 3 to 5 minutes more, or until the chicken is cooked through. Transfer to a plate.

5. Add the stock and miso to the pot over high heat, and bring to a boil. Add the udon and mushrooms. Continue cooking for 3 to 4 minutes. Remove from the heat.

6. To serve, divide the udon into 2 bowls. Top each bowl with half the chicken and sprinkle with scallions. Peel and place one egg into each bowl, then ladle the soup over top. Break the egg and enjoy.

ADD IT: Have leftover tofu in the fridge? Add it to this dish for extra flavor, texture, and protein. Simply cut the tofu into small cubes, then add with the udon and mushrooms in step 5.

Per Serving: Calories: 645; Total fat: 18g; Total carbs: 70g; Protein: 50g; Fiber: 7g; Sugar: 11g; Sodium: 2568mg

slow
cooker

serves
2

SWEET 'N' TANGY
SHREDDED CHICKEN SANDWICH

COMFORT FOOD
PREP TIME: 10 MINUTES / COOK TIME: 4 OR 8 HOURS,
DEPENDING ON COOKING METHOD

This shredded chicken sandwich is just as robust as it sounds, and it's super easy to make. The slow cooker does most of the hard work and intensifies the flavor, so every bite tantalizes your taste buds. The shredded chicken can be made ahead of time and stored in the freezer for up to two weeks.

2 (4-ounce) skinless boneless chicken breasts or thighs, cut into big pieces

½ cup maple syrup

¼ cup apple cider vinegar

¼ cup canned tomato paste

1 tablespoon Dijon mustard

½ small onion, diced

2 garlic cloves, minced

1 tablespoon extra-virgin olive oil

Salt

Freshly ground black pepper

4 butter lettuce leaves

2 brioche rolls or potato rolls, halved horizontally

1. In a slow cooker, combine the chicken, syrup, vinegar, tomato paste, mustard, onion, garlic, and olive oil. Season with salt and pepper. Toss to coat the chicken. Cover, and cook on high for 4 hours, or on low for 8 hours.

2. Remove the lid and shred the chicken with 2 forks.

3. Place 2 butter lettuce leaves on each roll. Add a spoonful of shredded chicken over the lettuce, then top the sandwich with the other half of the roll.

COOKING TIP: To make this on the stove, bring a pot of water to a boil. Add the chicken and cook for 8 to 12 minutes, until cooked through. Let cool before shredding. Add the oil to the pot. Cook the onion and garlic for 2 to 3 minutes. Add the chicken, syrup, vinegar, tomato paste, and mustard to the pot. Season with salt and pepper. Cook for 3 to 5 minutes, tossing to coat. Assemble as directed.

Per Serving: Calories: 553; Total fat: 13g; Total carbs: 81g; Protein: 31g; Fiber: 3g; Sugar: 52g; Sodium: 284mg

BRUSCHETTA GRILLED CHICKEN

GLUTEN-FREE
PREP TIME: 15 MINUTES / COOK TIME: 25 MINUTES

This low-carb sheet pan dinner gets its flavor from the cheesy mozzarella and classic Italian seasonings, while the tomatoes and basil add a fresh punch.

3 tablespoons extra-virgin olive oil, divided

½ teaspoon paprika

½ teaspoon Italian seasoning

Salt

2 (4-ounce) chicken breast cutlets

2 mozzarella cheese slices

2 ripe tomatoes, sliced

2 tablespoons chopped fresh basil

½ tablespoon balsamic vinegar, divided

Lemon wedges, for serving

1. In a bowl, combine 2 tablespoons of oil with the paprika and Italian seasoning, and season with salt. Whisk to combine. Transfer to a resealable bag with the chicken, seal and refrigerate for at least 15 minutes.

2. Preheat the oven to 400°F.

3. Remove the chicken from the marinade and let the excess liquid run off. Lay the cutlets on a baking sheet and bake for 15 to 20 minutes, or until the cutlets are fully cooked when you can cut into the centers and the juices run clear. Top each cutlet with 1 slice of mozzarella. Return to the oven and bake for 2 to 3 minutes, or until the mozzarella cheese is melted.

4. Place 1 tomato with 1 tablespoon of basil on each plate. Drizzle each with ¼ tablespoon of balsamic vinegar and ½ tablespoon of oil. Season with salt. Arrange chicken cutlets on top and serve with lemon wedges.

ADD IT: To add a more pungent flavor to the chicken, try it with 1 sliced red onion and 1 seeded, sliced bell pepper. In a medium bowl, combine the onion and pepper with 1 tablespoon of olive oil, salt, pepper, and a sprig of parsley. Place the vegetables around the chicken on the baking sheet and bake as directed.

Per Serving: Calories: 410; Total fat: 29g; Total carbs: 6g; Protein: 34g; Fiber: 2g; Sugar: 4g; Sodium: 336mg

SRIRACHA GLAZED CHICKEN

GLUTEN-FREE
PREP TIME: 10 MINUTES, PLUS MARINATING TIME /
COOK TIME: 40 MINUTES

My husband will put Sriracha on anything and everything. So when I pull out the ingredients to make this recipe, I earn some serious points. This tangy and spicy chicken, paired with delicious roasted sweet potatoes, is a delicious all-in-one meal perfect for a cozy weekend night in.

½ teaspoon garlic powder

½ cup gluten-free
 soy sauce

1 tablespoon honey

½ tablespoon rice
 wine vinegar

1 tablespoon Sriracha

½ teaspoon grated peeled
 fresh ginger

1 teaspoon sesame oil

Salt

2 (8-ounce) boneless
 skin-on chicken breasts

1 large sweet potato,
 peeled and cut
 into wedges

1 tablespoon extra-virgin
 olive oil

1 scallion, sliced,
 for garnish

1. In a large bowl, combine the garlic powder, soy sauce, honey, vinegar, Sriracha, ginger, and sesame oil, and season with salt. Mix until well combined. Spoon 1 tablespoon of the marinade out of the bowl to another small bowl, and set aside for glazing.

2. Add the chicken to the marinade, cover, and marinate for 30 minutes or more in the fridge.

3. Preheat the oven to 425°F.

4. Place the chicken in the center of a baking sheet, skin side up.

5. In a medium bowl, toss the sweet potatoes with the oil and salt, to coat. Arrange the potatoes in a single layer around the chicken on the pan. Roast for 15 minutes. Flip the potatoes, and roast for 15 to 20 minutes more, until the chicken is cooked through. Remove from the oven and let the chicken cool for 5 minutes. Brush the remaining marinade on top of each chicken breast.

6. Place 1 chicken breast and half the sweet potatoes on each plate. Garnish the chicken with scallions.

SWAP IT: Try this dish with 2 (6- to 8-ounce) salmon fillets, skins on. Marinate the salmon for 30 minutes to 1 hour. Bake the potatoes for 15 minutes at 425°F, then flip the potatoes, add the salmon to the pan, and cook for 15 more minutes, until cooked through. Brush with glaze and serve as directed.

Per Serving: Calories: 467; Total fat: 22g; Total carbs: 18g; Protein: 51g; Fiber: 2g; Sugar: 6g; Sodium: 316mg

PARMESAN-CRUSTED CHICKEN WITH SKILLET KALE

GLUTEN-FREE

PREP TIME: 10 MINUTES / COOK TIME: 20 MINUTES

When I first moved out on my own, Parmesan-crusted chicken was one of my favorite things to make. It's delicious, and you need only one skillet and virtually no effort to make it. Dinner's done before you know it.

1 tablespoon, plus
  1 teaspoon extra-virgin
  olive oil, divided

2 garlic cloves, minced

1 large bunch kale,
  coarsely chopped

Salt

Freshly ground
  black pepper

2 (4-ounce) chicken
  breast cutlets

2 egg whites,
  lightly beaten

1 cup grated
  Parmesan cheese

1 tablespoon butter

4 lemon wedges,
  for serving

1. Heat 1 tablespoon of the olive oil in a skillet over medium heat. Add the garlic and cook for 2 to 3 minutes, until fragrant.

2. Add the kale, a handful at a time, stirring as it starts to wilt, 1 to 2 minutes. Add salt and pepper to taste, and continue cooking until the kale is tender, about 5 minutes. Remove from the skillet and set aside. Wipe out the skillet with a paper towel.

3. Dip each chicken cutlet in the egg whites, then press the cutlets in the Parmesan cheese, turning to coat.

4. Heat the skillet on medium heat. Add the butter and the remaining 1 teaspoon of oil. When the butter melts, add the cutlets and cook about 5 minutes on each side, until golden brown and cooked through.

5. Divide the kale between 2 plates and top each with a chicken cutlet. Serve with lemon wedges.

Per Serving: Calories: 522; Total fat: 29g; Total carbs: 18g; Protein: 52g; Fiber: 2g; Sugar: 0g; Sodium: 812mg

serves
2

BAKED STUFFED CHICKEN SALTIMBOCCA

COMFORT FOOD
PREP TIME: 15 MINUTES / COOK TIME: 20 MINUTES

My husband and I make dinner most nights, so letting someone else do the cooking is a treat. This recipe is my version of the dish I always get when eating out. It's so easy to make that you can pretend you didn't cook at all.

Nonstick cooking spray

2 (6-ounce) chicken cutlets, pounded flat

Salt

Freshly ground black pepper

2 prosciutto slices

2 sage leaves, chopped

2 thin fresh mozzarella slices

1 cup Italian seasoned bread crumbs

½ cup grated Parmesan cheese, divided

1 egg, slightly beaten

1½ cups broccoli florets

1 tablespoon extra-virgin olive oil

4 lemon wedges, for squeezing

1. Preheat the oven to 425°F.

2. Spray a baking sheet with nonstick cooking spray.

3. Sprinkle each cutlet with salt and pepper. On each cutlet, lay 1 slice of prosciutto, 1 sage leaf, and 1 slice of mozzarella. Starting from the short end, roll the chicken up, and secure with toothpicks.

4. On a plate, combine the bread crumbs with ¼ cup of the Parmesan cheese. Dip the chicken in the egg, then in the bread crumbs mixture, turning to coat. Place the chicken on the middle of the prepared baking sheet.

5. Toss the broccoli with the olive oil, the remaining ¼ cup of Parmesan cheese, and salt and pepper to taste. Arrange the broccoli around the chicken on the baking sheet.

6. Bake for 18 to 20 minutes, until the chicken is cooked through and no longer pink.

7. Place a piece of chicken and half the broccoli on each plate. Squeeze 2 lemon wedges over each piece of chicken, and serve.

Per Serving: Calories: 756; Total fat: 29g; Total carbs: 48g; Protein: 76g; Fiber: 5g; Sugar: 5g; Sodium: 2120mg

BRAISED CHICKEN CACCIATORE

PREP TIME: 15 MINUTES / COOK TIME: 30 MINUTES

When I find recipes with little prep time, few ingredients, and awesome taste, I file them in my mind's "make again" section. That's exactly how I'd categorize this chicken cacciatore. The white wine makes it unique, and it's so easy to prepare in a Dutch oven.

Salt

Freshly ground
  black pepper

2 (4-ounce) boneless,
  skinless chicken breasts
  or thighs

½ tablespoon
  all-purpose flour

1 tablespoon extra-virgin
  olive oil

2 garlic cloves, crushed

1 small bell pepper, seeded
  and sliced

½ small onion, diced

⅓ cup white wine

1 cup canned crushed
  tomatoes

¼ cup chicken stock

4 ounces thin
  spaghetti noodles

1 tablespoon grated
  Parmesan cheese,
  for serving

1. Salt and pepper the chicken, and toss it in the flour to lightly coat.

2. Heat the oil in a Dutch oven over medium heat. Add the chicken and brown, about 5 minutes per side. Remove from the heat and set aside.

3. Add the garlic, bell pepper, and onion, and season with salt. Cook, stirring occasionally, for 3 to 4 minutes.

4. Add the wine and bring to a simmer. Cook until the liquid is reduced by half, about 8 minutes.

5. Add the tomatoes and stock. Adjust the salt to taste.

6. Add the spaghetti and return the chicken to the pot. Bring the sauce to a simmer, cover, and cook for 15 to 20 minutes, until the pasta is cooked and the chicken is tender. Stir again.

7. Divide between 2 plates and serve with grated Parmesan cheese.

SWAP IT: Don't have white wine on hand? Feel free to substitute red wine instead.

Per Serving: Calories: 554; Total fat: 11g; Total carbs: 63g; Protein: 45g; Fiber: 7g; Sugar: 13g; Sodium: 460mg

MEDITERRANEAN ONE-POT CHICKEN AND RICE

GLUTEN-FREE

PREP TIME: 10 MINUTES / COOK TIME: 30 MINUTES

This dinner is brimming with flavor from garlic, oregano, and olives. It's a one-pot meal that is truly restaurant quality. When paired with a nice bottle of wine, it becomes a standout dinner worthy of special company.

2 boneless skinless chicken breasts, cut into bite-size pieces

Salt

1 teaspoon dried oregano

¼ teaspoon garlic powder

¼ teaspoon ground turmeric

1 tablespoon extra-virgin olive oil

½ cup frozen peas

1 cup basmati rice, rinsed

1 cup chicken broth

1 dry bay leaf

½ cup pitted Greek olives, halved (optional)

1 tablespoon chopped fresh parsley, for garnish

1. Pat the chicken dry and season well with the salt, oregano, garlic powder, and turmeric.

2. Heat the oil in a pot over medium-high heat. Add the chicken and brown briefly on both sides, about 5 minutes.

3. Add the peas and rice to the pot. Cook for 2 minutes, stirring frequently, until the peas are tender.

4. Add the chicken broth and bay leaf, and bring to a boil. Turn the heat to low, cover, and cook for 20 minutes, until the rice is fully cooked.

5. Remove from the heat. Remove the bay leaf, stir in the olives (if using), and garnish with parsley to serve.

Per Serving: Calories: 591; Total fat: 10g; Total carbs: 81g; Protein: 42g; Fiber: 4g; Sugar: 2g; Sodium: 241mg

CHICKEN ENCHILADA CASSEROLE

COMFORT FOOD
PREP TIME: 10 MINUTES / COOK TIME: 30 MINUTES

With only 10 minutes of prep time, this casserole is perfect for busy week-nights. The chipotle gives this dish its smokiness. And don't forget the yummy garnishes!

Nonstick cooking spray

½ small onion, diced

1 cup canned black beans, drained and rinsed

½ cup frozen corn kernels, thawed and drained

1 tablespoon chipotle in adobo, seeded and minced

1 cup tomato sauce

½ teaspoon ground cumin

½ cup chicken stock

Salt

6 small (6-inch) flour tortillas, cut into 6 triangles each

1 cup shredded or diced cooked chicken

1 cup shredded Mexican four-cheese blend

1 jalapeño pepper, sliced, for garnish (optional)

Sour cream, for garnish (optional)

1 tablespoon chopped fresh cilantro, for garnish (optional)

1. Preheat the oven to 375°F.

2. Spray a casserole dish with nonstick cooking spray.

3. In a bowl, combine the onion, black beans, corn, chipotle, tomato sauce, cumin, and stock, and season with salt. Mix well.

4. Layer 12 tortilla triangles in the bottom of the casserole dish, overlapping each tortilla. Top with half the chicken, black bean mixture, and ⅓ cup of the cheese. Repeat the layers one more time, and top with the remaining 12 tortilla triangles.

5. Cover with aluminum foil and bake for 20 minutes. Uncover, sprinkle with the remaining ⅓ cup of cheese and bake for 5 to 10 minutes more, until cheese is melted and bubbly. If desired, garnish with jalapeño pepper, sour cream, and cilantro to serve.

SWAP IT: You can use cooked turkey meatballs instead. Dice the meatballs and replace the chicken with meatballs in step 4. You can also swap in jarred salsa for the tomato sauce.

Per Serving: Calories: 478; Total fat: 24g; Total carbs: 72g; Protein: 48g; Fiber: 17g; Sugar: 8g; Sodium: 1379mg

TURKEY STUFFED PEPPER CASSEROLE

PREP TIME: 15 MINUTES / COOK TIME: 45 MINUTES

What could be better than a dump-and-bake meal for dinner on a busy weeknight? This filling, Mexican-inspired casserole has all the great flavors of stuffed peppers, but without the extra fuss of stuffing them.

Nonstick cooking spray

1 large bell pepper, any color, seeded, diced

½ cup frozen corn

¼ cup uncooked long-grain white rice

½ small onion, diced

½ pound ground turkey

1 cup beef broth

¼ cup tomato sauce

2 garlic cloves, minced

1 chipotle in adobo, seeded and minced

Salt

Freshly ground black pepper

¼ cup shredded Mexican four-cheese blend

¼ cup tortilla chips, crushed, for garnish

1 tablespoon chopped fresh cilantro, for garnish

1. Preheat the oven to 375°F.

2. Spray a casserole dish with nonstick cooking spray.

3. In the dish, add the bell pepper, corn, rice, and onion. Break up the ground turkey into small pieces with your hands and sprinkle over the top. Use your hands to gently combine the mixture.

4. In a medium bowl, whisk together the broth, tomato sauce, garlic, and chipotle, and season with salt and pepper. Pour over the turkey mixture. Cover with aluminum foil and bake for 30 minutes.

5. Remove the foil, stir, and cover again. Bake for an additional 10 minutes, or until the meat, rice, and vegetables are fully cooked and tender.

6. Uncover and sprinkle with the cheese. Bake, uncovered, for 3 to 5 minutes more, until the cheese is melted. Garnish with tortilla chips and cilantro to serve.

Per Serving: Calories: 382; Total fat: 16g; Total carbs: 42g; Protein: 31g; Fiber: 5g; Sugar: 7g; Sodium: 1002mg

CREAMED TURKEY WITH TARRAGON CASSEROLE

COMFORT FOOD
PREP TIME: 15 MINUTES / COOK TIME: 35 MINUTES

This ravioli casserole is smothered in a rich homemade Alfredo sauce—and cheese. It's a great way to use up any Thanksgiving turkey leftovers. You can substitute cooked chicken, if that's what you have on hand.

FOR THE SAUCE

3 tablespoons unsalted butter

2 tablespoons all-purpose flour

1½ cups milk

1 tablespoon dry white wine

¼ cup Parmesan cheese

Salt

FOR THE CASSEROLE

1 (8-ounce) package frozen wild mushroom ravioli

1 cup cooked turkey, cut into thin strips

½ cup frozen peas, thawed

½ cup diced carrot

1 tablespoon fresh tarragon, chopped

½ cup shredded Italian cheese blend

2 tablespoons Parmesan cheese

1. Preheat the oven to 400°F.

2. To make the sauce, melt the butter in a Dutch oven over medium heat, and add the flour while the butter warms. Stir until the flour is fully blended into the butter. Slowly whisk in the milk and wine. Sprinkle in the Parmesan cheese and salt to taste, and stir the sauce until slightly thickened. Turn off the heat.

3. To make the casserole, ladle out most of the sauce into a bowl, leaving the bottom of the Dutch oven coated in a layer of sauce.

4. Arrange half the ravioli in a single layer over the sauce. Layer ½ cup of the turkey on top. Sprinkle the peas, carrot, and tarragon over the turkey. Add half of the remaining sauce and top with ¼ cup of the Italian cheese.

5. Add the remaining ravioli and ½ cup of turkey on top of the cheese, and pour on the remaining sauce. Top with the remaining ¼ cup of Italian cheese and sprinkle the Parmesan cheese on top.

6. Cover with aluminum foil and bake for 20 minutes. Remove the foil and bake, uncovered, for 15 minutes more, or until the casserole is bubbly and hot in the center. Serve warm.

PREP HACK: This dish, uncooked, freezes wonderfully. Make the sauce in the Dutch oven, but assemble the casserole following steps 3 through 5 in a casserole dish. Wrap in plastic wrap, pressing down to remove any air. Cover with foil and freeze. To prepare, thaw in the fridge overnight. Bake, covered, for 30 minutes at 400°F; then bake uncovered for 15 minutes, or until it is golden on top and bubbling.

Per Serving: Calories: 807; Total fat: 43g; Total carbs: 51g; Protein: 53g; Fiber: 5g; Sugar: 13g; Sodium: 861mg

Meat

GRILLED PROSCIUTTO AND MOZZARELLA SANDWICH

SUPER QUICK
PREP TIME: 10 MINUTES / COOK TIME: 20 MINUTES

The idea for this sandwich had been floating around in my head for a while. When I finally made it, the taste exceeded my expectation.

1 tablespoon extra-virgin
   olive oil

1 cup brown
   mushrooms, sliced

1 cup spinach leaves

Salt

4 sourdough bread slices

1 teaspoon Dijon mustard

1 cup arugula

1 cup fresh mozzarella, cut
   into thin slices

4 prosciutto slices

1 tablespoon
   unsalted butter

1. Heat the olive oil in a skillet over medium heat. Add the mushrooms and sauté for 5 minutes, stirring occasionally. Add the spinach and cook, stirring occasionally, for 2 to 3 minutes. Season with salt and set aside. Wipe the skillet clean with a paper towel.

2. Place 2 bread slices on a work surface or plate. Spread ½ teaspoon of mustard on each slice, and arrange half the arugula and a quarter of the mozzarella cheese on each slice. Top each with half the mushroom-spinach mixture, 2 slices of prosciutto, and another quarter of the cheese. Top with bread slices.

3. Heat the skillet over medium heat and melt the butter. Place a sandwich in the center of the skillet. Cover, and cook for 4 to 5 minutes, until golden brown on the bottom. Flip the sandwich and press lightly with a spatula. Cover, and cook for 3 to 4 minutes, until the bottom is golden brown and the cheese has melted.

4. Transfer to a plate and cut the sandwich in half. Repeat with the other sandwich.

Per Serving: Calories: 606; Total fat: 32g; Total carbs: 41g; Protein: 40g; Fiber: 2g; Sugar: 3g; Sodium: 1957mg

MINCED PORK LETTUCE CUPS

SUPER QUICK, GLUTEN-FREE
PREP TIME: 10 MINUTES / COOK TIME: 10 MINUTES

This leaner version of the traditional Chinese dish can accommodate a variety of meats or meat substitutes. Minced chicken, lean beef, and tofu are all delicious options! Because this low-carb recipe is packed with protein and fresh vegetables, it makes for a healthy meal that will leave you feeling full and satisfied, but not heavy. Feel free to add other diced or julienned vegetables to the lettuce cups.

1 tablespoon sesame oil

2 garlic cloves, minced

½ tablespoon grated or chopped ginger

½ pound lean ground pork

1 tablespoon hoisin sauce

1 tablespoon gluten-free soy sauce

Salt

Freshly ground black pepper

1 cup bean sprouts, trimmed

8 butter lettuce leaves

½ cup canned water chestnuts, chopped

1 tablespoon chopped roasted peanuts

1. Heat the oil in a skillet over medium heat. Add the garlic and ginger, and cook, stirring frequently, for 2 to 3 minutes.

2. Add the pork and cook for 5 minutes, until pork just changes color. Add the hoisin sauce and soy sauce, and season with salt and pepper. Cook, stirring, for 2 to 3 minutes, then remove from the heat.

3. On a plate, place a small pile of bean sprouts in each lettuce leaf. Top with the pork mixture, water chestnuts, and peanuts.

SWAP IT: Water chestnuts are sold in both the Asian and canned vegetable sections of major supermarkets, but if you can't find them, swap for diced fresh jicama. The flavor might be different, but you will still get the crunchy texture of the chestnuts.

Per Serving: Calories: 433; Total fat: 34g; Total carbs: 11g; Protein: 22g; Fiber: 1g; Sugar: 3g; Sodium: 662mg

PORK ZOODLE RAMEN

GLUTEN-FREE
PREP TIME: 15 MINUTES / COOK TIME: 20 MINUTES

The tenderest zoodles I've ever made were boiled in broth. These zoodles in miso broth will keep you warm and full during the fall season. If you can't find bone broth, you can substitute any broth or stock you have on hand. Like a bit of spice? Drizzle the finished dish with Sriracha.

2 large eggs

2 tablespoons extra-virgin olive oil

2 garlic cloves, minced

½ pound ground pork

½ tablespoon gluten-free soy sauce

1 teaspoon white miso paste

4 cups low-sodium bone broth

Salt

1 cup cremini mushrooms, sliced

2 medium zucchini, spiralized

2 cups spinach

1 scallion, sliced, for garnish

1 teaspoon sesame oil

1. Boil a medium pot of water. Add the eggs, and cook for 6 minutes. Using a slotted spoon, transfer the eggs to a large bowl filled with cold water. Let cool, then peel and set aside.

2. Discard the water from the pot and wipe dry. Heat the olive oil in the pot over medium heat. Add the garlic and cook for 2 to 3 minutes, stirring frequently. Add the pork and soy sauce, stirring to break up meat slightly, about 3 minutes. Set aside.

3. Add the miso to the pot, and cook for 1 minute. Stir in the bone broth, and salt to taste. Add the mushrooms. Cover, and bring to a low boil. Uncover, reduce the heat to medium, and simmer for 5 minutes. Add the zoodles and spinach, and cook for 1 minute. Remove from the heat.

4. Divide the zoodles and spinach between 2 bowls. Top evenly with the soup, ground pork, and egg, and garnish with scallion. Drizzle with sesame oil to serve.

> **PREP HACK:** Don't have a spiralizer? You can make zoodles using a vegetable peeler to cut strips from the zucchini.

Per Serving: Calories: 817; Total fat: 60g; Total carbs: 13g; Protein: 52g; Fiber: 3g; Sugar: 5g; Sodium: 675mg

BRAISED PORK TACOS

GLUTEN-FREE
PREP TIME: 15 MINUTES / COOK TIME: 8 HOURS

Picture this: You've had a long day. The last thing you feel like doing is making a meal. You suddenly remember you have braised pork in a slow cooker waiting for you. Wrap it in a tortilla, and you have a complete meal. Breathe a sigh of relief—victory is yours tonight!

½ (10-ounce) can
  tomato sauce

½ teaspoon chipotle in
  adobo, minced

½ teaspoon ground cumin

½ teaspoon brown sugar

2 garlic cloves, smashed
  and peeled

½ pound boneless pork
  shoulder, fat trimmed

Salt

Freshly ground
  black pepper

½ small onion, thinly sliced

¼ cup water

4 small (6-inch) corn
  tortillas, warmed

1 small avocado, sliced
  (optional)

1 cup thinly sliced cabbage
  (optional)

1 tablespoon chopped
  fresh cilantro (optional)

4 lime wedges for
  squeezing and garnish
  (optional)

1. In a slow cooker, add the tomato sauce, chipotle, cumin, brown sugar, and garlic. Mix well.

2. Cut the pork shoulder into 4 equal pieces and season generously with salt and pepper. Add the pork, onion, and water to the slow cooker. Cover, and cook on low for 7 to 8 hours. Transfer the pork shoulder to a cutting board, and let cool slightly. Shred the pork into bite-size pieces, discarding excess fat.

3. Serve with warm tortillas, the sauce from the slow cooker, and, if desired, top with the avocado, cabbage, cilantro, and lime juice and garnish with lime wedges.

COOKING TIP: To make this in a Dutch oven, add 1 tablespoon of olive oil over medium-high heat. Brown the meat on all sides until a golden crust forms, 8 to 10 minutes. Transfer to a plate. Cook the garlic and onion for 5 minutes, until soft. Add the tomato sauce, chipotle, cumin, brown sugar, and stir for 1 minute. Return the pork to the pot, then stir in the water. Cover and cook at 325°F for 2½ hours, and shred.

Per Serving: Calories: 256; Total fat: 5g; Total carbs: 29g; Protein: 25g; Fiber: 5g; Sugar: 5g; Sodium: 804mg

SMOKED SAUSAGE GUMBO

COMFORT FOOD
PREP TIME: 20 MINUTES / COOK TIME: 8 HOURS

Spice up your dinner with this amazing gumbo recipe. A slow cooker makes this version of the Creole classic a breeze. This dish is the perfect thing to eat while watching the game on the couch at home.

1 (14½-ounce) can diced tomatoes, undrained

1 cup chicken stock

¼ cup all-purpose flour

2 smoked sausages, sliced ½-inch thick

1 (6-ounce) skinless boneless chicken breast, cut into bite-size pieces

1 small onion, diced

1 small bell pepper, diced

1 celery rib, chopped

1 cup sliced okra

1 teaspoon Creole seasoning

Pinch salt

¼ teaspoon freshly ground black pepper

1 scallion, sliced (optional)

1. Turn on the slow cooker to high. Add the canned tomatoes, with juice, and stock. Sprinkle the flour evenly over the top and cook, without stirring, for 3 to 4 minutes. Whisk to combine.

2. Add the sausage, chicken, onion, bell pepper, celery, okra, Creole seasoning, salt, and pepper to the cooker. Stir well, cover, and cook on low for 7 to 8 hours.

3. Ladle the gumbo into 2 bowls and serve with sliced scallions (if using).

COOKING TIP: To make this on the stovetop, melt 1 tablespoon of unsalted butter in a Dutch oven over medium heat. Cook the sausage and chicken for 6 minutes, or until browned. Drain on paper towels. Add the flour and cook, whisking constantly, about 15 minutes. Stir in the onion, bell pepper, celery, and okra and cook until tender. Gradually add the stock, tomatoes, seasoning, salt, and pepper. Bring to a simmer, stirring occasionally, for 30 minutes. Serve as directed.

Per Serving: Calories: 459; Total fat: 22g; Total carbs: 34g; Protein: 33g; Fiber: 6g; Sugar: 11g; Sodium: 1608mg

LAZY LASAGNA

COMFORT FOOD

PREP TIME: 10 MINUTES / COOK TIME: 45 MINUTES

On hectic nights, who has time to boil lasagna noodles, make a meat sauce, and then layer the components? This version cuts down on prep and takes some shortcuts with no-boil noodles and jarred marinara sauce. It can easily be doubled to feed a crowd.

½ cup ricotta cheese

½ cup shredded
  mozzarella cheese

1 cup jarred marinara sauce

9 ounces no-boil
  lasagna noodles

2 Italian sausages, sliced

2 tablespoons fresh
  basil, sliced

2 tablespoons grated
  Parmesan cheese

1. Preheat the oven to 375°F.

2. In a medium bowl, combine the ricotta and mozzarella cheeses.

3. In the bottom of a casserole dish, spread ⅓ cup of the marinara sauce. Layer half of the lasagna noodles on top, then spread half of the cheese mixture, half of the sausage, and 1 tablespoon of the fresh basil on top of the noodles. Repeat the layering process once more, then top with the remaining ⅓ cup of marinara sauce.

4. Bake, uncovered, for 35 minutes, until the noodles are fork-tender. Sprinkle with the Parmesan cheese and bake for another 7 to 8 minutes or until cheese is melted and bubbly. Serve warm.

SWAP IT: Try swapping the lasagna noodles for 1 (9-ounce) package fresh ravioli.

Per Serving: Calories: 659; Total fat: 22g; Total carbs: 75g; Protein: 41g; Fiber: 5g; Sugar: 5g; Sodium: 1091mg

BEEF NACHOS

COMFORT FOOD

PREP TIME: 10 MINUTES / COOK TIME: 20 MINUTES

I have never met a nacho I didn't like. These beef nachos are easy to make as well as delicious and filling. This dish is a weekend favorite in our house. Not a fan of beer? Simply replace it with beef stock.

1 tablespoon extra-virgin olive oil

¼ small onion, sliced

½ pound ground beef

1 teaspoon dried oregano

½ teaspoon cumin

½ teaspoon garlic powder

Salt

½ cup Mexican beer, such as Tecate

Freshly ground black pepper

6 ounces tortilla chips (about ½ bag)

½ cup Monterey Jack cheese, for serving

1 jalapeño pepper, sliced, for serving

1 small Roma tomato, diced, for serving

2 lime wedges, for squeezing

1. Turn on your electric pressure cooker and set to sauté. Add the oil and onion to the pot, and cook for 3 minutes, until the onion is tender.

2. Add the ground beef, oregano, cumin, garlic powder, and season with salt. Cook, stirring occasionally, for 5 minutes. Pour in the beer.

3. Close and lock the lid, and cook on high pressure for 10 minutes. Quick release the pressure. Turn off the cooker, open the lid, and season with salt and pepper.

4. On a platter, spread an even layer of chips, then top with the ground beef, Monterey Jack cheese, jalapeño pepper, tomato, and squeeze lime wedges on top to serve.

COOKING TIP: To make the beef topping on the stove, add oil to a pot over medium-high heat. Cook the onion for 3 to 5 minutes. Add the ground beef, oregano, cumin, garlic powder, and season with salt. Cook, stirring occasionally for 5 minutes. Add beer and cook for 10 minutes, or until cooked through. Season with salt and pepper.

Per Serving: Calories: 858; Total fat: 53g; Total carbs: 56g; Protein: 43g; Fiber: 6g; Sugar: 3g; Sodium: 667mg

GROUND BEEF STROGANOFF

COMFORT FOOD
PREP TIME: 10 MINUTES / COOK TIME: 30 MINUTES

I don't know about you, but when I am craving a comforting home-cooked meal that can be prepared in minutes, stroganoff is where my mind goes. This hamburger gravy over egg noodles is budget friendly as well as easy to make—what could be better?

1 large shallot, thinly sliced

1 cup fresh
    mushrooms, sliced

2 tablespoons
    unsalted butter

½ pound lean ground beef

1 tablespoon
    all-purpose flour

2 cups beef broth

1 tablespoon
    Worcestershire sauce

Salt

Freshly ground
    black pepper

1 cup wide egg noodles

2 tablespoons sour cream

1 tablespoon chopped
    fresh parsley, for garnish

1. Heat a Dutch oven over medium-high heat. Add the shallot, mushrooms, and butter. Cook until the mushrooms have softened, about 3 minutes. Set aside.

2. Add the beef and cook, stirring to break up the meat, until browned and no longer pink, 5 to 6 minutes. Drain off most of the fat, leaving about 1 tablespoon.

3. Reduce the heat to medium. Return the mushrooms to the pot. Sprinkle the flour over the mushrooms and beef, stirring until the flour is fully mixed in.

4. Add the broth and Worcestershire sauce, and season with salt and pepper. Stir to combine. Increase the heat to medium-high and bring to a gentle boil.

5. Add the egg noodles and stir to combine. Cover and simmer, stirring occasionally, for 10 to 12 minutes, until the noodles are tender and the liquid is absorbed.

6. Remove from the heat and add the sour cream. Stir to coat evenly. Sprinkle with parsley to garnish, and serve.

Per Serving: Calories: 489; Total fat: 32g; Total carbs: 21g; Protein: 29g; Fiber: 1g; Sugar: 3g; Sodium: 781mg

SLOPPY JOE POTATOES

GLUTEN-FREE
PREP TIME: 15 MINUTES / COOK TIME: 30 MINUTES

When you scan the ingredients in this recipe, you know it's going to be a winner. Think of it as a less-fancy version of steak and potatoes.

2 small russet potatoes

2 tablespoons unsalted butter

Salt

Freshly ground black pepper

½ pound 90% lean ground beef

2 tablespoons diced onion

2 tablespoons diced green bell pepper

1 garlic clove, minced

½ cup canned tomato sauce

1 teaspoon Worcestershire sauce

1 scallion, sliced, for garnish (optional)

1. Wash and dry the potatoes. Poke each potato with a fork a few times.

2. In a Dutch oven over medium heat, melt the butter. Add the potatoes and season with salt and pepper. Reduce the heat to low. Cover and cook, turning the potatoes occasionally to prevent sticking or burning, for 15 minutes, until the potatoes are tender when poked with a fork. Transfer the potatoes to a bowl.

3. In the Dutch oven over medium heat, sauté the beef, onion, bell pepper, and garlic, until beef is no longer pink, about 10 minutes.

4. Stir in the tomato sauce and Worcestershire sauce, and season with salt and pepper. Bring to a boil and turn off the heat.

5. To serve, slit the potatoes down the middle and spoon the sloppy joe mixture over the potato. Garnish with scallions (if using).

COOKING TIP: Slow cookers are great for making saucy recipes, and you can make this sloppy joe mixture ahead of time. Just combine all the ingredients in a slow cooker, except for the potatoes, and cook on low for 8 hours, or on high for 4 hours.

Per Serving: Calories: 253; Total fat: 25g; Total carbs: 41g; Protein: 34g; Fiber: 7g; Sugar: 12g; Sodium: 597mg

BALSAMIC-GLAZED STEAK WRAPS

SUPER QUICK, 5-INGREDIENT
PREP TIME: 10 MINUTES / COOK TIME: 10 MINUTES

I love steak and I love wraps, and this recipe is the perfect marriage of the two. After seeing a few different steak roll-up recipes on Pinterest, I thought I'd try my own version. I'm so glad I did! This recipe can be made on the stovetop, as shown here, or on the grill.

3 tablespoons
  balsamic vinegar

Salt

Freshly ground
  black pepper

2 (4-ounce) beef tenderloin
  filet mignon steaks,
  fat trimmed

2 tablespoons extra-virgin
  olive oil

4 flour tortillas

8 butter lettuce leaves

2 small tomatoes, sliced

1. In a dish, combine the balsamic vinegar, salt, and pepper. Place the steaks in the marinade and allow to stand for 3 minutes on each side.

2. Heat the oil in a Dutch oven over medium-high heat. Add the steaks and cook for 3 minutes on each side, until browned. Transfer the steaks to a plate and let cool for 10 minutes. Slice the steaks.

3. Divide the tortillas between 2 plates. Add 2 butter lettuce leaves to each tortilla, and top with sliced tomatoes and steak. Fold over and enjoy.

USE IT AGAIN: Have extra butter lettuce on hand? Make Minced Pork Lettuce Cups (see page 113).

Per Serving: Calories: 421; Total fat: 23g; Total carbs: 26g; Protein: 29g; Fiber: 4g; Sugar: 3g; Sodium: 170mg

SHEET PAN STEAKHOUSE DINNER

COMFORT FOOD

PREP TIME: 10 MINUTES / COOK TIME: 30 MINUTES

Midweek meals don't get much better than this sheet pan dinner. The perfectly seasoned, melt-in-your-mouth steak with potatoes and broccoli comes together in a snap and is fancy enough for a special occasion.

Nonstick cooking spray

½ pound baby red potatoes, halved

2 cups broccoli florets

2 tablespoons extra-virgin olive oil

1 teaspoon garlic powder

2 tablespoons grated Parmesan cheese

Salt

Freshly ground black pepper

2 (8-ounce) New York strip steaks, about 1-inch thick

2 tablespoons butter, melted

1 teaspoon minced fresh basil

1 garlic clove, minced

1. Preheat the oven to 425°F.

2. Spray a baking sheet with nonstick cooking spray.

3. In a bowl, combine the potatoes and broccoli with the oil, garlic powder, and Parmesan cheese, and season with salt and pepper. Toss to coat well. Arrange the potatoes and broccoli in a single layer on the prepared pan. Bake for 20 minutes, until golden brown and crisp, tossing occasionally. Remove from the oven, and transfer the potatoes and broccoli to a plate, and tent with foil to keep warm.

4. Preheat the oven to broil. Season the steaks by rubbing salt and pepper on both sides. Place on the baking sheet. Broil for 4 to 5 minutes per side for medium-rare, or until desired doneness. Remove the steaks from the oven and let rest for 10 minutes before slicing.

5. While the steaks are resting, in a small bowl, whisk together the melted butter, basil, and garlic, and season with salt.

6. Divide the potatoes and broccoli between 2 plates. Add 1 sliced steak to each plate and drizzle with melted butter to serve.

SWAP IT: Looking to add a different flavor to this dish? Use cubed sweet potatoes instead of baby red potatoes.

Per Serving: Calories: 649; Total fat: 35g; Total carbs: 28g; Protein: 58g; Fiber: 5g; Sugar: 3g; Sodium: 428mg

PRESSURE COOKER BEEF STEW

COMFORT FOOD
PREP TIME: 15 MINUTES / COOK TIME: 30 MINUTES

Beef stew is one of the best things to make in an electric pressure cooker because of how quickly it can tenderize tough cuts of meat. This easy, hearty recipe delivers a rich and flavorful sauce and fall-apart beef, carrots, and potatoes.

3 tablespoons
all-purpose flour

1 tablespoon Italian
seasoning, divided

Salt

Freshly ground
black pepper

½ pound beef stew meat,
cut into 1-inch chunks

1 tablespoon extra-virgin
olive oil

2 garlic cloves, minced

½ tablespoon red
wine vinegar

1 tablespoon tomato paste

½ cup diced carrot

½ cup diced celery

1 large potato, peeled,
chopped into
1-inch chunks

1 cup beef broth

1 tablespoon
Worcestershire sauce
(optional)

1 cup water

½ tablespoon chopped
fresh parsley, for garnish
(optional)

1. In a resealable bag, combine the flour, ½ table-spoon of the Italian seasoning, and season with salt and pepper. Add the beef, close the bag, and shake until well coated.

2. Set the electric pressure cooker to sauté or brown. Heat the oil. Brown the meat on all sides, taking care not to crowd the pot, about 5 to 8 minutes. Transfer to a plate.

3. Add the garlic to the pot and sauté for 2 minutes. Add the red wine vinegar and tomato paste, and using a wooden spoon or spatula, scrape the bottom to deglaze the pot, getting all the brown bits.

4. Return the beef to the pot and add the carrot, celery, potato, the remaining ½ tablespoon of Italian seasoning, beef broth, Worcestershire sauce (if using), and water. Stir to combine. Cover, and cook for 20 minutes on high pressure. Allow the pressure to release naturally, about 10 minutes.

5. Turn off the cooker, open the lid, and season with salt and pepper. Ladle the stew into 2 bowls and serve hot with parsley for garnish (if using).

COOKING TIP: To make this on the stovetop, follow step 1 and set aside. Heat oil over medium-high heat. Add the meat and brown on all sides. Remove to a plate. Sauté the garlic for 2 minutes. Add the red wine vinegar and tomato paste and deglaze the pot. Cook for 2 minutes. Return the beef, along with the ingredients in step 4, to the pot. Stir to combine and cook for 30 minutes. Season with salt and pepper. Serve as directed.

Per Serving: Calories: 374; Total fat: 14g; Total carbs: 31g; Protein: 29g; Fiber: 4g; Sugar: 5g; Sodium: 247mg

LAMB KEBABS WITH ISRAELI SALAD

GLUTEN-FREE
PREP TIME: 20 MINUTES / COOK TIME: 20 MINUTES

Lamb doesn't have to be tied up, roasted rare, and served on a china platter. I like to take a less stuffy approach: I use ground lamb to make kebabs.
I love kebabs because they marinate and cook super fast. Served with a
salad of fresh veggies on the side, these kebabs make a winning dish on
a warm summer night. If you have leftovers, stuff the lamb and salad in a
warm pita with a drizzle of hot sauce or tahini for lunch the next day. Yum!

¼ pound ground lamb

¼ pound ground beef

3 garlic cloves, minced

1 small onion, grated

2 tablespoons minced
    chipotle in adobo

½ cup roughly chopped
    fresh cilantro

Salt

Freshly ground
    black pepper

4 tablespoons extra-virgin
    olive oil, divided

2 cups chopped
    fresh parsley

1 tomato, seeded and
    finely diced

1 large cucumber, peeled,
    seeded, and finely diced

1 tablespoon freshly
    squeezed lemon juice

½ cup fresh mint leaves,
    for garnish

1. Preheat the oven to 350°F.

2. In a bowl, combine the ground lamb and beef,
   garlic, onion, chipotle, and cilantro, and season
   with salt and pepper. Mix until well combined.
   Divide the mixture into 8 equal portions. Use
   the palms of your hands to form each portion
   into a 4-by-1-inch oval patty. Insert a skewer
   lengthwise through each patty.

3. Place the kebabs on a baking sheet. Drizzle with 1 tablespoon of olive oil, turning the skewers to evenly coat the meat. Bake for 18 to 20 minutes, until cooked through, flipping once halfway through cook time. Transfer the kebabs to a platter.

4. To make the salad, combine the parsley, tomato, cucumber, the remaining 3 tablespoons olive oil, lemon juice, and salt to taste. Garnish with mint leaves. Serve cool or room temperature, with the lamb kebabs.

COOKING TIP: To make these patties on the stovetop, heat a skillet over medium-high. Add the lamb patties (without skewers), and cook until deep golden brown on each side, 4 to 5 minutes. Flip and continue cooking until meat is cooked through.

Per Serving: Calories: 577; Total fat: 48g; Total carbs: 19g; Protein: 26g; Fiber: 8g; Sugar: 6g; Sodium: 532mg

SLOW COOKER BRISKET

GLUTEN-FREE
PREP TIME: 15 MINUTES, PLUS MARINATING TIME / COOK TIME: 8 HOURS

The hardest part about this recipe is waiting for it to be done. As you know, any meat cooked in the slow cooker will be tender, and this brisket doesn't disappoint. It's not easy to find a brisket smaller than 1½ pounds, so you'll have leftovers unless you divide the brisket and freeze one half. Add the brisket to a toasted bun and—voilà!—you have a brisket sandwich.

1 teaspoon garlic powder

1 teaspoon onion powder

1 teaspoon oregano

Salt

Freshly ground
    black pepper

1½ pounds beef brisket,
    trimmed of excess fat

½ small onion, thinly sliced

2 garlic cloves, minced

1 cup beef broth

½ cup red wine (optional)

1 tablespoon gluten-free
    soy sauce

1 large carrot, sliced

1 cup mixed mushrooms

1 tablespoon chopped
    fresh parsley, for garnish

1. In a small bowl, mix the garlic powder, onion powder, and oregano, and season with salt and pepper. Rub evenly over the surface of the brisket. Put the brisket in a large, resealable plastic bag, and refrigerate for 30 minutes, to overnight.

2. Add the brisket to a slow cooker. Add the onion, garlic, beef broth, red wine (if using), and soy sauce. Cover, and cook on low for 7 hours, until fork-tender. Add the carrot and mushrooms, and continue cooking 1 hour more.

3. Transfer the brisket onto a wood cutting board, cover with foil, and let rest for 20 minutes. Slice the meat against the grain and serve with the sauce and vegetables from the slow cooker. Garnish with parsley to serve.

COOKING TIP: To make in a Dutch oven, brown the marinated brisket with 1 tablespoon of olive oil over medium heat, 8 to 10 minutes. Remove the brisket, add another tablespoon of oil, and cook the onion and garlic for about 10 minutes. Add the brisket, broth, red wine, and soy sauce, and cook for 3 hours at 300°F or until fork-tender. Serve as directed.

Per Serving: Calories: 530; Total fat: 21g; Total carbs: 11g; Protein: 74g; Fiber: 2g; Sugar: 4g; Sodium: 589mg

8

Snacks and Sides

SAUTÉED GARLIC-BUTTER MUSHROOMS

SUPER QUICK, 5-INGREDIENT, GLUTEN-FREE, VEGETARIAN
PREP TIME: 10 MINUTES / COOK TIME: 10 MINUTES

In addition to their wonderful complex taste, mushrooms are packed with good-for-you nutrients. They are the perfect addition to soups, stews, and even cooked rice, but they stand alone very well, too. In this easy recipe, mushrooms are sautéed in garlic butter with a hint of herbs. Serve them as a side for Parmesan-Crusted Chicken with Skillet Kale (see page 102).

2 tablespoons
  unsalted butter
2 garlic cloves, minced
½ pound fresh
  mushrooms, halved
  (cremini, oyster, shiitake,
  white button, or a mix)
2 thyme or rosemary sprigs
Salt
Freshly ground
  black pepper
1 tablespoon chopped
  fresh parsley, for garnish

1. In a skillet over medium heat, melt the butter. Add the garlic and cook for 2 minutes.

2. Stir in the mushrooms and thyme, and cook for 5 to 7 minutes, until mushrooms are browned and tender. Season with salt and pepper, and sprinkle with parsley to garnish. Discard herb sprigs. Serve immediately.

Per Serving: Calories: 131; Total fat: 12g; Total carbs: 5g; Protein: 4g; Fiber: 1g; Sugar: 2g; Sodium: 167mg

THREE-MINUTE CORN ON THE COB

SUPER QUICK, 5-INGREDIENT, GLUTEN-FREE, VEGETARIAN
PREP TIME: 5 MINUTES / COOK TIME: 3 MINUTES

There's nothing that says summer like sweet corn on the cob with melted butter on top. I know, cooking corn on the cob is not rocket science. But three minutes? You won't want to wait for water to boil on the stove ever again. This corn makes a great side dish for a summer cookout with friends.

1 cup water

2 ears corn, husks and silk removed

½ tablespoon unsalted butter, melted

½ tablespoon grated Parmesan cheese

½ teaspoon chopped fresh parsley

Salt

Freshly ground black pepper

1. Pour the water into an electric pressure cooker and insert a steamer basket. Place the corn in the basket. Close and lock the lid, and cook on high pressure for 3 minutes. Quick release the pressure.

2. Turn off the cooker, open the lid carefully, and remove the corn to a plate. To serve, brush the corn with the melted butter and sprinkle with the Parmesan cheese, parsley, salt, and pepper.

COOKING TIP: To make this on the stove, fill a large pot with water and bring to a boil. Add the corn, cover, reduce heat to medium, and cook 8 to 10 minutes or to desired tenderness. Season as directed.

Per Serving: Calories: 93; Total fat: 4g; Total carbs: 14g; Protein: 3g; Fiber: 2g; Sugar: 2g; Sodium: 125mg

CREAMED CORN

5-INGREDIENT, COMFORT FOOD, GLUTEN-FREE, VEGETARIAN
PREP TIME: 10 MINUTES / COOK TIME: 2 OR 4 HOURS, DEPENDING
ON COOKING METHOD

The slow cooker is my absolute favorite vessel for making the creamiest corn. This dish would make a delicious side for a Friday night Sheet Pan Steakhouse Dinner (see page 122).

2 cups frozen corn kernels

¼ cup whole milk

Salt

Freshly ground
black pepper

½ cup cream
cheese, cubed

2 tablespoons
unsalted butter

½ teaspoon chopped fresh
parsley, for garnish

1. In a slow cooker, add the corn and milk, and season with salt and pepper. Stir until combined, then top with the cream cheese and butter. Cover and cook on high for 2 hours, or low for 4 hours. Stir the corn every hour to prevent a crust from forming.

2. Stir, and adjust the salt and pepper to taste. Garnish with parsley to serve.

Per Serving: Calories: 393; Total fat: 34g; Total carbs: 17g; Protein: 8g; Fiber: 2g; Sugar: 9g; Sodium: 348mg

CAJUN POPCORN

SUPER QUICK, 5-INGREDIENT, GLUTEN-FREE, VEGETARIAN
PREP TIME: 5 MINUTES / COOK TIME: 10 MINUTES

This popcorn is destined to be your new favorite TV snack. Embrace a Southern theme and enjoy it on the couch with a movie after your dinner of Shrimp 'n' Grits (see page 80).

3 tablespoons extra-virgin olive oil

⅓ cup high-quality popcorn kernels

1 tablespoon unsalted butter, melted

1 teaspoon lemon pepper

1 teaspoon Cajun seasoning

1. Heat the oil in a pot on medium-high heat. Add 3 to 5 popcorn kernels to the oil. When the kernels pop, add the rest of the popcorn kernels in an even layer. Cover, remove from the heat, and let sit for 30 seconds.

2. Return the pan to the heat. Once the popping starts in earnest, gently shake the pan, moving it back and forth over the burner. Once the popping slows to several seconds between pops, remove the pan from the heat and pour the popcorn into a bowl.

3. In a small bowl, combine the melted butter with the lemon pepper and Cajun seasoning. Pour over the popcorn and toss to coat. Serve and enjoy!

SWAP IT: Make this Mexican Popcorn instead! Swap the Cajun seasoning and lemon pepper for ¼ teaspoon each of garlic powder, onion powder, cumin, paprika, chili powder, and a pinch of salt in a bowl. Mix with the butter and sprinkle over the popcorn, tossing to coat.

Per Serving: Calories: 255; Total fat: 27g; Total carbs: 5g; Protein: 1g; Fiber: 1g; Sugar: 0g; Sodium: 66mg

ROASTED CHICKPEAS

GLUTEN-FREE, VEGAN
PREP TIME: 5 MINUTES / COOK TIME: 35 MINUTES

When you have a craving for something crispy to nosh on, try these chickpeas—they are going to change the way you think about snacking!

1 (15-ounce) can chickpeas, drained and rinsed

1 teaspoon extra-virgin olive oil

1 teaspoon garlic powder

1 teaspoon onion powder

1 teaspoon dried parsley

½ teaspoon paprika

Salt

Freshly ground black pepper

1. Preheat the oven to 450°F.

2. In a bowl, toss the chickpeas with the olive oil, garlic powder, onion powder, parsley, and paprika, and season with salt and pepper.

3. Spread on a baking sheet and bake for 30 to 35 minutes, until browned and crunchy. Serve immediately.

Per Serving: Calories: 232; Total fat: 6g; Total carbs: 36g; Protein: 11g; Fiber: 10g; Sugar: 7g; Sodium: 88mg

GARLIC-HERB PINWHEELS

SUPER QUICK, 5-INGREDIENT, COMFORT FOOD, VEGETARIAN
PREP TIME: 10 MINUTES / COOK TIME: 15 MINUTES

sheet pan

serves
2

This great grab-and-go snack can be stored in an airtight container at room temperature for up to three days.

¼ cup mixed fresh herbs, such as parsley, basil, and chives

2 garlic cloves, minced

2 tablespoons unsalted butter, melted

Salt

Freshly ground black pepper

All-purpose flour, for dusting

1 frozen puff pastry sheet, thawed but still cold

1 tablespoon grated Parmesan cheese

1. In a small bowl, combine the fresh herbs, garlic, and butter. Season with salt and pepper.

2. Unfold the puff pastry on a lightly floured work surface. Spread the butter mixture evenly over the dough. Sprinkle the puff pastry with the Parmesan cheese. Roll up tightly to make a log and place in the freezer for 10 to 15 minutes.

3. Preheat the oven to 400°F.

4. Line a baking sheet with parchment paper.

5. With a sharp knife, cut the log into ½-inch-thick rounds. Arrange the rounds on the prepared baking sheet and bake until puffed and the edges are golden, about 15 minutes. Let cool for 10 minutes before serving.

ADD IT: Take these pinwheels to another level by adding some thinly sliced prosciutto on top of the Parmesan before rolling up.

Per Serving: Calories: 582; Total fat: 44g; Total carbs: 40g; Protein: 7g; Fiber: 2g; Sugar: 1g; Sodium: 388mg

CHEESY SESAME LAVASH CRISPS

SUPER QUICK, 5-INGREDIENT, VEGETARIAN
PREP TIME: 5 MINUTES / COOK TIME: 10 MINUTES

Lavash is a soft, thin unleavened flatbread. Enjoy this recipe as a snack, or serve it as an accompaniment to Lamb Kebabs with Israeli Salad (see page 126).

½ cup grated
  Parmesan cheese

1 teaspoon onion powder

1 tablespoon white
  sesame seeds

3 teaspoons extra-virgin
  olive oil, divided

2 lavash pieces, each about
  9 inches by 10 inches

1 teaspoon extra-virgin
  olive oil

Salt

1. Preheat the oven to 425°F.

2. In a small bowl, combine the Parmesan cheese, onion powder, sesame seeds, and 1 teaspoon of the olive oil.

3. Place the lavash on a baking sheet. Brush the 2 pieces with 1 teaspoon of oil each, and generously season with the cheese mixture. Toast in the oven until crisp and golden, about 10 minutes. Let cool completely on the baking sheet before breaking into pieces to serve.

SWAP IT: You can replace lavash with pita bread. Cut each pita into quarters and then each quarter to halves to make 8 triangles. Arrange and season as directed. Bake at 400°F for about 10 minutes, until crisp.

Per Serving: Calories: 370; Total fat: 15g; Total carbs: 43g; Protein: 17g; Fiber: 2g; Sugar: 1g; Sodium: 641mg

DEVILISH DEVILED EGGS

SUPER QUICK, GLUTEN-FREE, VEGETARIAN
PREP TIME: 5 MINUTES / COOK TIME: 15 MINUTES

Although deviled eggs are typically served to a crowd, there's no reason the two of you can't enjoy them as a snack or breakfast. Of course, if you're having friends over for game day or a party, you can double, triple, or even quadruple the recipe!

2 large eggs

1 tablespoon mayonnaise

1 teaspoon Dijon mustard

1 teaspoon hot sauce, such as Sriracha

Salt

Freshly ground black pepper

Cayenne pepper, for garnish

½ teaspoon chives, finely chopped, for garnish

1. Fill a pot with enough water to cover the eggs and bring to a full boil. Boil, uncovered, for about 30 seconds. Reduce the heat to low and cover. Simmer for 12 minutes. Transfer the boiled eggs to a bowl of ice water. When the eggs are cool enough to handle, gently break the shells apart and peel.

2. Cut the boiled eggs in half. Separate the yolks from the whites using a teaspoon.

3. In a bowl, combine the egg yolks, mayonnaise, mustard, and hot sauce, and season with salt and pepper. Fill a piping bag or resealable bag with mixture, cut off one corner of the bag, then squeeze the mixture into the halves of the boiled eggs.

4. Garnish with sprinkles of cayenne pepper and chives to serve.

PREP HACK: You can make deviled eggs up to 2 days in advance. Just store the whites and egg yolk filling separately. Wrap the egg white halves well with plastic wrap and keep the egg yolk filling sealed in a resealable plastic bag with all the air squeezed out, until ready to assemble and serve.

Per Serving: Calories: 102; Total fat: 8g; Total carbs: 2g; Protein: 7g; Fiber: 0g; Sugar: 1g; Sodium: 292mg

DIJON POTATO SALAD

GLUTEN-FREE, VEGETARIAN
PREP TIME: 10 MINUTES / COOK TIME: 35 MINUTES

This creamy potato salad is one of my family's favorite side dishes. The Dijon mustard and red onion give it zip. With this recipe, you reap a big reward for very little effort.

2 large red potatoes, peeled or unpeeled, cut into 1½-inch chunks

1 large egg

2 tablespoons mayonnaise

1 teaspoon Dijon mustard

½ cup finely chopped celery

¼ cup finely chopped red onion

Salt

Freshly ground black pepper

1 teaspoon chopped chives

1. Bring a pot of salted water to a boil. Add the potatoes and cook until tender, about 15 minutes. Transfer the potatoes to a large bowl and refrigerate for 20 minutes.

2. Place the egg in the pot and bring to a boil. Reduce the heat to medium and gently boil, uncovered, for 8 minutes. Drain and run cold water over the egg until it is cool enough to handle. Peel, chop, and set aside to cool further.

3. In a bowl, combine the mayonnaise, mustard, celery, and red onion. Add the potatoes and chopped eggs. Season with salt and pepper, and toss gently to combine. Sprinkle with chives to serve.

ADD IT: Give your potato salad a kick with a squeeze or two of Sriracha or other hot sauce, or make it meaty with ½ cup of diced, crispy bacon.

Per Serving: Calories: 389; Total fat: 8g; Total carbs: 70g; Protein: 11g; Fiber: 9g; Sugar: 5g; Sodium: 288mg

GARLIC-PARMESAN
SMASHED POTATOES WITH BACON

GLUTEN-FREE, VEGETARIAN
PREP TIME: 10 MINUTES / COOK TIME: 35 MINUTES

Smashed potatoes are the perfect side to just about any dish, but they can also serve as a main. Bacon adds crunch, and garlic and onion add kick.

2 tablespoons grated
 Parmesan cheese

¼ teaspoon garlic powder

¼ teaspoon onion powder

1 teaspoon chopped
 fresh parsley

Salt

½ pound small round or
 fingerling potatoes

3 bacon slices, cut into
 ½-inch pieces

Freshly ground
 black pepper

1. In a small bowl, mix the Parmesan cheese, garlic powder, onion powder, and parsley. Set aside.

2. Fill a Dutch oven with water and sprinkle with salt. Add the potatoes. Bring to a boil and simmer for about 15 minutes, until soft. Drain, and remove the potatoes, and set aside.

3. Add the bacon to the Dutch oven over medium-high heat. Cook, flipping occasionally, until crisp, about 8 minutes. Remove the bacon, and let drain on a paper towel–lined plate. Crumble into pieces when cool.

4. Arrange half the potatoes in the Dutch oven over medium-high heat, leaving room in between them. Cook until golden and crispy, about 5 minutes. Set aside and repeat the same process with the remaining potatoes.

5. Use a potato masher to lightly flatten each potato, keeping it together. Season with salt and black pepper, and sprinkle with the bacon pieces and parsley mixture to serve.

SWAP IT: Swap the parsley for fresh rosemary for a deeper flavor.

Per Serving: Calories: 258; Total fat: 14g; Total carbs: 19g; Protein: 15g; Fiber: 3g; Sugar: 2g; Sodium: 809mg

SESAME SWEET POTATO FRIES

GLUTEN-FREE, VEGAN
PREP TIME: 10 MINUTES / COOK TIME: 35 MINUTES

This sesame seed spin on sweet potato fries is simply sensational.

Nonstick cooking spray
2 medium sweet potatoes
2 tablespoons cornstarch
4 tablespoons extra-virgin
   olive oil, divided
2 tablespoons maple syrup
2 teaspoons gluten-free
   soy sauce
2 teaspoons rice
   wine vinegar
1 teaspoon miso paste
Salt
2 teaspoons white
   sesame seeds

1. Preheat the oven to 425°F.

2. Spray a baking sheet with nonstick cooking spray.

3. Peel the sweet potatoes and slice them into
   thin, fry-shaped pieces. Use a paper towel to
   blot away any excess moisture.

4. Place the sweet potatoes in a large bowl. Add
   the cornstarch and 1 tablespoon of oil, and
   toss to coat. Spread the potatoes on an even
   layer on the prepared baking sheet. Bake for
   20 minutes.

5. While the potatoes are baking, combine the
   maple syrup, soy sauce, vinegar, miso paste,
   and the remaining oil in a bowl. Add salt
   to taste. Pour the mixture over the sweet
   potato fries, and toss to coat. Bake for another
   15 minutes, until the fries are crispy. Sprinkle
   with sesame seeds and enjoy.

Per Serving: Calories: 232; Total fat: 15g; Total carbs: 24g;
Protein: 2g; Fiber: 2g; Sugar: 9g; Sodium: 317mg

serves
2

BEST FRENCH FRIES WITH CHIPOTLE MAYO

SUPER QUICK, COMFORT FOOD, GLUTEN-FREE, VEGETARIAN
PREP TIME: 10 MINUTES / COOK TIME: 30 MINUTES

....

"The best?" you ask. I believe these French fries really are. They require little effort, and the dipping sauce puts them over the top.

....

FOR THE FRENCH FRIES
4 cups vegetable oil
2 large russet potatoes, cut into ¼-inch sticks
Salt

FOR THE SAUCE
½ cup mayonnaise
4 tablespoons minced chipotle in adobo
2 tablespoons freshly squeezed lime juice
½ teaspoon garlic powder
Salt
Freshly ground black pepper

1. To make the French fries, heat the oil in a Dutch oven over high heat. When the oil has heated, dip the handle of a wooden spoon or a chopstick into the oil. If the oil starts steadily bubbling, then it is hot enough for frying. If the oil bubbles very vigorously, then the oil is too hot and needs to cool a bit. Gently put the potatoes in the oil and cook for 15 minutes without stirring. Use a pair of tongs and gently scrape loose any stuck potatoes after 15 minutes. Continue to cook, stirring when necessary, for 5 to 10 minutes, or until crisp and golden. Use a large slotted spoon to remove the potatoes and spread them on a brown paper bag or paper towel–lined tray to cool. Season with salt.

2. To make the sauce, combine the mayonnaise, chipotle, lime juice, and garlic powder, and season with salt and pepper. Mix well with a fork until well combined and smooth. Serve and enjoy.

USE IT AGAIN: Have extra sauce? Use it to top Garlic-Lime Fish Tacos (see page 85). It'll keep in the fridge for up to a week.

Per Serving: Calories: 403; Total fat: 25g; Total carbs: 43g; Protein: 5g; Fiber: 5g; Sugar: 4g; Sodium: 621mg

Snacks and Sides   143

BACON CHEESEBURGER DIP

COMFORT FOOD, GLUTEN-FREE
PREP TIME: 10 MINUTES / COOK TIME: 30 MINUTES

What's more American than a cheeseburger? This recipe is a no-brainer to celebrate Memorial Day and the Fourth of July! Loaded with bacon, Swiss cheese, and cream cheese, this dip is not for the diet conscious, but if you want a comfort food treat, there's nothing better.

2 bacon slices, cut into ¼-inch pieces

½ cup diced onion

½ pound lean ground beef

Salt

Freshly ground black pepper

4 ounces cream cheese

2 tablespoons water

1 cup shredded Swiss cheese

1 tomato, diced

1 teaspoon chopped fresh parsley

2 jalapeño peppers, seeded and sliced

2 ounces tortilla chips, for serving

1. Turn on the sauté mode on an electric pressure cooker, and add the bacon. Cook for 10 minutes, until crisp. Transfer the bacon to a small bowl.

2. Add the onion to the pressure cooker and cook for 3 to 5 minutes. Add the ground beef and, breaking apart the meat, cook for 7 minutes, or until no longer pink. Season with salt and pepper. Turn off the pot and drain off the excess grease.

3. Add the cream cheese and water to the pot. Cover, and cook on high pressure for 5 minutes. Quick release the pressure. Add the Swiss cheese and stir until everything is well combined, and transfer the dip into a bowl.

4. Top with bacon, tomato, parsley, and jalapeño peppers, and serve with tortilla chips.

> **COOKING TIP:** To cook in a Dutch oven, add the bacon to a cold Dutch oven then turn heat to low. Once the bacon starts to brown, flip and continue cooking until crispy, about 10 minutes. Remove the bacon, and drain off the bacon grease, reserving 1 tablespoon. Increase heat to medium-high, and cook the onion and beef as directed. Season with salt and pepper and stir in the cheeses and water. Bake in a 375°F oven for 10 minutes, or until golden and bubbly.

Per Serving: Calories: 826; Total fat: 58g; Total carbs: 28g; Protein: 50g; Fiber: 3g; Sugar: 4g; Sodium: 996mg

Measurement Conversions

VOLUME EQUIVALENTS (LIQUID)

US STANDARD	US STANDARD (OUNCES)	METRIC (APPROXIMATE)
2 tablespoons	1 fl. oz.	30 mL
¼ cup	2 fl. oz.	60 mL
½ cup	4 fl. oz.	120 mL
1 cup	8 fl. oz.	240 mL
1½ cups	12 fl. oz.	355 mL
2 cups or 1 pint	16 fl. oz.	475 mL
4 cups or 1 quart	32 fl. oz.	1 L
1 gallon	128 fl. oz.	4 L

OVEN TEMPERATURES

FAHRENHEIT (F)	CELSIUS (C) (APPROXIMATE)
250°F	120°C
300°F	150°C
325°F	165°C
350°F	180°C
375°F	190°C
400°F	200°C
425°F	220°C
450°F	230°C

VOLUME EQUIVALENTS (DRY)

US STANDARD	METRIC (APPROXIMATE)
1/8 teaspoon	0.5 mL
¼ teaspoon	1 mL
½ teaspoon	2 mL
¾ teaspoon	4 mL
1 teaspoon	5 mL
1 tablespoon	15 mL
¼ cup	59 mL
1/3 cup	79 mL
½ cup	118 mL
2/3 cup	156 mL
¾ cup	177 mL
1 cup	235 mL
2 cups or 1 pint	475 mL
3 cups	700 mL
4 cups or 1 quart	1 L
½ gallon	2 L
1 gallon	4 L

WEIGHT EQUIVALENTS

US STANDARD	METRIC (APPROXIMATE)
½ ounce	15 grams
1 ounce	30 grams
2 ounces	60 grams
4 ounces	115 grams
8 ounces	225 grams
12 ounces	340 grams
16 ounces or 1 pound	455 grams

The Dirty Dozen™ and the Clean Fifteen™

A nonprofit environmental watchdog organization called Environmental Working Group (EWG) looks at data supplied by the US Department of Agriculture (USDA) and the Food and Drug Administration (FDA) about pesticide residues. Each year, EWG compiles a list of the best and worst pesticide loads found in commercial crops. You can use these lists to decide which fruits and vegetables to buy organic to minimize your exposure to pesticides and which produce is considered safe enough to buy conventionally. This does not mean they are pesticide-free, though, so wash these fruits and vegetables thoroughly. The list is updated annually, and you can find it online at EWG.org/FoodNews.

DIRTY DOZEN™

> apples	> kale	> potatoes
> celery	> nectarines	> spinach
> cherries	> peaches	> strawberries
> grapes	> pears	> tomatoes

†Additionally, nearly three-quarters of hot pepper samples contained pesticide residues.

CLEAN FIFTEEN™

> asparagus	> cauliflower	> mushrooms
> avocados	> sweet corn*	> onions
> broccoli	> eggplants	> papayas*
> cabbages	> kiwis	> sweet peas (frozen)
> cantaloupes	> melons, honeydew	> pineapples

* A small amount of sweet corn, papaya, and summer squash sold in the United States is produced from genetically modified seeds. Buy organic varieties of these crops if you want to avoid genetically modified produce.

Recipe Index by Cooking Vessel

Index

Acknowledgments

A huge thank you to the Callisto Media editorial and design team who supported me throughout this project and helped make it a wonderful reality. Ada, Patty, Melissa, Gleni, Tricia, and Sue—without you, this book would never have happened.

To my husband, Frederick, for always believing in me and supporting me all the way. My little munchkins, Gideon and Lindy, there are no words for the treasures you are. You are my true secret ingredients, and you make my life so unbelievably tasty! Thank you to my parents and family for your endless support and belief in this book. What began with a skillet and a spatula in August 1998 has turned into hundreds of recipes.

To my dear friends, Evelyn, Patrisia, and Lilia, thanks for always cheering me on and sending me photos of good food to make me drool. (And thanks to dark chocolate, for sustaining me through many long nights of writing.)

And last, but definitely not least, thanks to the Simply Healthyish Recipes community, without whom this book would not have been possible. Thank you for your excitement, positive feedback, and for being my internal sunshine! What a beautiful journey it's been!

About the Author

LINDA KURNIADI grew up in Indonesia before moving to San Francisco for her studies. Living so far from home, missing the flavors of her mom's cooking, and surviving on a student's budget, Linda was inspired to try out her own recipes and share them on her blog, Simply Healthyish Recipes.

To her delight, Linda could create delicious dishes that were zesty, healthy, comforting, and most importantly—simple to make. She was inspired to write *5-Ingredient One-Pot Cookbook: Easy Dinners from Your Skillet, Dutch Oven, Sheet Pan, and More* and is gratified she could follow up on its success with this book. Her recipes have been featured on MSN.com and theFeedFeed.com as well as in *Better Homes and Gardens* magazine, *Country Living* magazine, and *Taste of Home* magazine. To find more of Linda's recipes, visit SimplyHealthyish.com.